READER REVIE

M. Dodig: Former sergeant, 82nd Airborne, U.S. Army—I just finished reading **When I Was a Child.** Each chapter, each page, made me want to read more. It is a compelling story of a young man who grows up in western Kansas, loses his parents, is separated from his siblings, and eventually serves as a paratrooper in WWII. Ironically, it is his love of family that is the cornerstone of his life and the driver of the story. Having served as a paratrooper in the 82nd Airborne Division myself, I was especially intrigued by the war scenes, but this is not a war story. It's a human story, and the combat experience is merely one of the challenges in Louis Pfeifer's tumultuous life. Knowing that Louis was a real person, and that this is an account of his actual experiences, makes the story that much more engaging.

Twice is Nice – Jeanie: Lately I find that I can skip 3/4 of a book . . . and still get the point at the end and feel like I missed nothing, but this book was different. It required that you read each page and I found myself actually wanting to read and savor each page. Rarely does a book grip me from start to finish like this one did. This is the kind of book that begs you to pick it up and read just a little bit more each night, even though you are exhausted and really need your sleep. This book is a history buffs dream as it weaves family life and history into one. If you love history or just love to read "real" books with real family tragedies and triumphs, you will not be disappointed in this book.

Readers Favorite – Maureen: Wow! The author did a wonderful job of writing about his family. What a horrible life these poor children ended up having! The story is very powerful . . . Through all of this they keep their faith in God and family. This book is a page-turner and I highly recommend reading it . . .

Robert G Yokoyama: T. L. Needham's writing captures a reader's attention in the first few pages . . . I found myself caring about the people in this book like they were members of my own family . . . The writing in this book gives me a sense of how hard life really was back then . . . ***When I Was A Child*** is the best book of non-fiction I have read in a long time.

M. Plaskett: . . . a marvelous true story . . . ***When I Was a Child*** is so heart rendering, it will bring tears to your eyes while other parts of the book will put a smile on your face. Adversity builds character, which is apparent with the neglect and abuse suffered by the children in Needham's book, as they grow to become strong spiritual individuals. Plus the love of family is so compelling as Needham expresses through their hardships. The turmoil of war, the great depression, crisis of death, are all presented in eloquent fashion. Quite frankly, ***When I Was a Child*** would make a great movie. I will give this book this holiday season as gifts to friends and family so they can experience this wonderful masterpiece.

P. Hininger: T. L. Needham has graced us with an invitation to share the dramatic, sometimes riveting, history . . . Using historical details, literary techniques, and a good dose of creativity, Needham has delivered a smooth, well-crafted story taken from a real-life tale. He transports readers to a time when life itself was an adventure . . . flanked with blessings and hardships by both the hand of man and the will of God. *When I Was A Child* is a salute to . . . resilience and spirit, and a distinguished achievement for T. L. Needham.

K. Stehwien: I normally don't read a book in 2 days; I'm usually a casual reader. I couldn't put this book down.

Midwest Book Review: Through the roughest of challenges, survival always seems to be toughest of them . . . *When I Was A Child* is a touching and poignant read, highly recommended.

L. Bratta: Loved it!!! When I started reading *When I Was A Child*, I couldn't put it down and page after page kept me wanting to know what happened next to this Kansas family. I always thought Chicago winters were bad! I would recommend everyone read this book.

S. Dodig: You know a book is really good when you finish reading it and feel like you've just said good-bye to a dear friend . . . The reader is immediately pulled in and develops a personal connection. This story is inspiring to read and makes you realize the true inner strength that simply being deeply loved can give someone. I am so grateful for all the hours of enjoyment reading this book has brought me, and highly recommend it . . .

When I Was A Child

Based on a true story of love, death, and survival on the Kansas prairie.

T. L. Needham

Outskirts Press, Inc.
Denver, Colorado

Outskirts Press, Inc.
http://www.outskirtspress.com

ISBN: 978-1-4327-7136-2

Library of Congress Control Number: 2011923205

PRINTED IN THE UNITED STATES OF AMERICA

For Theresa

When I was a child, I spoke as a child,
I understood as a child, I thought as a child:
But when I became a man, I put away childish things.

First Corinthians 13:11

— This story was inspired by true events. —

Table of Contents

Foreword
A parachute lost and found xi

Chapter 1
Hey, Chief! Is this the flight to Chicago? 1

Chapter 2
Good-bye, Mother.. 15

Chapter 3
After the jump into hell...................................... 27

Chapter 4
A helluva night 33

Chapter 5
Guest of the Third Reich....................................47

Chapter 6
Front page news 59

Chapter 7
Why be a paratrooper?.. 65

Chapter 8
The Volga-Germans 73

Chapter 9
Haunted by hunger under the stars...................81

Chapter 10
Train ride to nowhere 87

Chapter 11
Back to the farm 109

Chapter 12
Stalag 4D – welcome to hell 123

Chapter 13
Windmills, tornados, and a runaway too 129

Chapter 14
Time to grow up fast 137

Chapter 15
Buckets of blood 141

Chapter 16
Father is accused 145

Chapter 17
Orphanage times 153

Chapter 18
Jerry goes, Louis stays 161

Chapter 19
Jerry meets Jack, love blooms 173

Chapter 20
Gene & Irene's 177

Chapter 21
POW liberation, at last! 185

Chapter 22
To trust, to hope, and to endure
whatever comes... 197

Chapter 23
Alex Pfeifer, the final years 209

Chapter 24
Martina becomes Sister Mary Vita 213

Chapter 25
Kewpie dolls for sale 219

Afterword 229

Sources..231

Acknowledgements 235

A parachute lost and found

My earliest memory of Uncle Louis was on the Fourth of July, 1948, at the Needham family picnic at Swope Park in Kansas City. We were picnicking and playing all day with wonderful fireworks after dark. My name is Terry Louis, named after my Uncle Louis, the World War II paratrooper and beloved brother of my mother, Geraldine, or Jerry as she was referred to by friends and family. That night I had recovered a parachute from one of the fireworks. It became a treasured relic of the day for me, a sickly, skinny, and asthmatic little four-year-old kid.

Driving home late that evening and well after dark, I am sitting in the back seat on my Uncle Louis' lap, holding my parachute out of the window. Dad is driving, Mom sits beside him. My baby sister Patty sits between Mom and Dad in front. My brother Charlie and sister Sue sit in back in the middle with our Aunt Gilberta sitting nearest to her husband, my Uncle Louis.

Holding my parachute out the window, watching it billow in the rushing air…it slips from my hand! I cried out, "Dad! Stop the car, I lost my parachute." Dad's only response was to speed up a little, in silent protest of my urgent request to interrupt the drive home for such a trivial reason. Dad is tired. It has been a long day, and he has to work tomorrow.

He always worked long, hard hours on the railroad.

Mom tries to intervene on my behalf, as she always had done. "Honey, aren't you going to stop the car?" Dad's silence and steady speed is his only response.

Suddenly, in an unexpected, but definitely adamant tone of voice, Uncle Louis demanded, "Jack! Stop the car!"

This demand was to my amazement, and everyone else in the car, because Dad was not someone you told what to do—no one! Dad actually did slow down the car, braked rather suddenly, and pulled the car over to the shoulder. With only the words "I'll be right back," Uncle Louis opened the door, got out of the car, and began to walk back down the road from where we came. Leaning out the window, wondering how, and if, he could ever find that tiny parachute in the darkness, and how far back into the darkness would he have to walk to find it, in silence, I watched as my Uncle Louis grew smaller and smaller…finally disappearing in the darkness.

After a long period of time, and heavy silence in the car, it seemed you could feel Dad fuming; with no one wanting to risk breaking the silence, we waited for Uncle Louis to return. Only I, hanging out the window, kept a hopeful, yet silent, vigil waiting and wondering. Then, as if a mere shadow or a ghost, he emerged from the darkness, swinging a small, square white cloth tied at each corner by four short strings to a washer the size of a quarter, which he held securely in his grasp. Whistling a curiously happy tune.

"My parachute! My parachute! Uncle Louie has it! He found my parachute, Mom, look!" I cried out.

Uncle Louis got back into the car after he'd laid the parachute into my outstretched hand. Dad started the car, put it in gear, and pulled out onto the road. No one said a word for several minutes. I sat there holding my treasured parachute relic in my hand, then stuck my head out the window again, put the parachute out into the air flow, holding tightly to the little washer, and ignored my dad when he finally said, "Roll up that damn window and hold tight on that parachute."

Uncle Louis whispered in my ear, "Your dad is right, hold on tight to that parachute. It may save your life someday." I did not, could not, fully understand the implication of what my Uncle Louis had just said. But I never forgot it, and years later, as I learned more about the story of his and my mother's childhood, the meaning became clearer to me. So, here is their story as I know it, inspired by the true and remarkable events of their lives during the 1920s to the 1940s—an era characterized by the tremendous twenties, the desperate thirties, and the fearsome forties. An era few generations have ever experienced or been challenged to endure.

— *T. L. Needham*

Private. Louis Pfeifer – 1942

Remember Me

If I should ever leave you,
And forget to say goodbye,
And you know I shall not return,
Don't let it make you cry.

Just know that I had business
In a place so far away,
Yet, close enough to you
To hear each word you pray.

And know that I am always near,
Though see me you may not,
But with you just the same
In your memory and thoughts.

And know I love you always,
So wherever you may be,
I shall always be there too
As long as you remember me.

— *T. L. Needham*

Jerry Pfeifer-Needham &
Louis Pfeifer, March 1943

Hey, Chief! Is this
the flight to Chicago?

Louis looked around the cabin at the other men on his stick of 17 paratroopers. This flight included a major, a 2nd lieutenant, two sergeants, two corporals, and eleven privates, including Louis. Each man had his face blacked for nighttime camouflage. They were all fully armed and each carried about 100 pounds of equipment. They were flying directly into war—it was just before midnight, June 5, 1944. Within about two hours they would each be fully committed into combat as part of the D-Day Invasion, June 6, 1944.

He knew these men. He had trained with these men for many months. He had laughed, played, and lived life with these men. He knew their names, the town they were from, and in most cases their wives' or girlfriends' names too—but he did not want to think about any of that now. Now he only wondered which of them would see the sunrise and which would not survive this night. He knew what they all knew—this plane ride might be a one-way ticket to hell for most, if not all, of them.

Louis glanced to his left, his buddy James' eyes met his,

both could see the somber dread in each other's eyes, and then they each laughed and shook their heads. The absurdity of it all—a plane trip into the unknown in the middle of the night, armed to the teeth, ready to give and take hell-fire. Prepared to jump out of an airplane into total darkness, into enemy territory to become the hunted, and to do their own hunting—except unlike the jackrabbits he hunted back home in Kansas, this time he would be hunting Germans. And the Germans would certainly be hunting them too.

"Hey, Chief! Is this the flight to Chicago?" James suddenly yelled at the sergeant jumpmaster sitting beside the door. The jumpmaster gave James a "thumbs-up" gesture and yelled back, "Sure, you bet, and your landing zone is second base at Wrigley Field!" Louis laughed and so did those who could hear the exchange over the deafening roar of hundreds of Douglas C-47 Pratt & Whitney engines taxiing for take off. The vibration alone made your teeth rattle, or was that fear welling up within? No way—just relax, enjoy the ride, Louis reassured himself.

For a brief moment the tension was relaxed and fleeting thoughts of home took over the cold sweat of fear he was feeling. Fear, but no doubt—he was determined and ready. He was in the First Battalion, Company B of the 507th Parachute Infantry Regiment of the 82nd Airborne Division of the United States Army—*and damn proud of it*. He knew his duty and the mission. If all hell was about to break out, he would be one of the men bringing hell down from the midnight sky onto the Germans below.

Finally, their C-47 pulled out onto the runway at

Fulbeck Airfield in Lincolnshire in northeastern England, and without a moment's delay the two engines roared to takeoff speed and the plane with its load of 82nd Airborne warriors began to race down the runway. Louis always liked that moment when the plane was suddenly airborne—the bumps and vibrations gave way to a sudden stillness and smoothness, with only the harmonic roar of the twin engines pulling the plane and its contents skyward.

That was it. Takeoff was over, they were in the air, committed to the mission, no turning back now. Whatever waited in the next hours was up to each man's personal destiny. But Louis did not dwell on such lofty ideas. In those moments after takeoff a dull monotony took over, and while some men actually napped, or at least pretended to, others fiddled with their gear, smoked cigarettes, and some just stared at the floor or the ceiling, or out the open jump door if your seat position allowed that view. But few talked, or looked at each other. Each alone with his own thoughts, knowing but not wanting to dwell on it: death awaits, and either you will deliver or receive that destiny. But it was clear that "kill or be killed" was the order of the day.

Each paratrooper knew his mission and the objective of the 507th. They had been briefed over and over in great detail in the days prior to this fateful mission. They trained over terrain boards that were miniature reproductions of the areas of their jump zones and were drilled many times each day on their objectives. Every action they were expected to take was reviewed in detail from the time they hit the ground.

Their objective was to parachute into Drop Zone "T" shortly after 0230 hours, then assemble into fighting units, seize and defend their objective area, and clear it of enemy resistance. Then move on to secure the crossing bridge of the Meredet River at La Fiere in concert with the 505th Parachute Infantry Regiment. Next, make contact with the 508 Parachute Infantry Regiment and join them in advancing to the west to secure the crossings of the Douve River. This was a bold and daring plan. It was well conceived and thought out by the command. Louis and his fellow paratroopers knew this and were confident in the success of their mission.

This entire airborne mission was a critical part of the Western Allies' D-Day invasion of the Normandy coast of German-occupied France. The airborne assault behind the beaches was to secure river crossings and control them to hinder the Germans from moving reinforcements toward the coast once the attack was underway. It would also control access to the inland routes as the beachhead at Normandy was established and Allied troops continued their assault inland.

Louis let his mind wander back over his life. The early days on the farm in Hays, Kansas. That one hellish night that changed everything. The good days living with his Grandma Pfeifer, along with his beloved big sister Geraldine, or "Jerry" as he had always affectionately referred to her, who always took care of him. Then the days back on the farm after Grandma's death. Another horrible time, with lives tossed to the winds of fate. Then St. Joseph's orphanage in Abilene, Kansas. Finally the days back in Hays with his oldest brother Gene and his family. So much more, but the one constant in all the upheaval and uncertainty of his childhood was his sister Jerry. She had taken her little brother under her wing even before their mother died. He was her responsibility, delegated by their beloved mother, and if Jerry did anything, she took care of her responsibilities. Yet more than that, Jerry was the one constant source of love in Louis' life. His grounded sense of family—that no matter what happened, we were family and we take care of each other—was always the message given by Jerry's love for him.

Louis wondered where Jerry was at this moment; what was she doing? It would be early in the evening in Kansas City. She probably was just making dinner for her husband Jack and their two children, Charlie and Sue. Then Louis reminded himself that Jerry was also expecting another child very soon—July as he recalled. Louis wondered if the blessings of family life waited for him down the road. His thoughts moved on to what his father was like—a paradox of good and bad, a very hard man, who could also be so loving and gentle too—and his own difficult life. Louis promised himself that if he survived this war and found the right woman, he would be as good a husband and father as any man ever was....

As the planes loaded with paratroopers approached the coast of the Cotentin Peninsula of Normandy in France, distant booming explosions began to be heard over the roar of the engines. From his seat Louis could see out the open jump door and the armada of C-47s flying in formation toward the coast of France. The air-burst explosions were now felt like bumps or concussions in the air, as the shock wave of each explosion radiated out in all directions. Now Louis could see flashes of light, and then feel the bumps as masses of clouds and dense fog also began to rush past the open jump door. The fog and dense overcast sky was not part of the plan and would not help this mission, Louis thought. Jumping out of an airplane in daylight with clear sky was one thing. Jumping out at night in total darkness was something else. But jumping out at night into a thick cloud with no sense of where the ground was or what awaited down below—land, water, a German encampment…whatever? But never dwell on fear, Louis thought. The only way out of this airplane was out that jump door, and whatever waited down below was what he had been trained to deal with and was well prepared to face. This was his mission, his job, and his duty.

However, Louis' sense of calm and confidence began to fade and chill as the reality of possible death at any moment became the new and obviously real possibility. He looked around at the other men for a brief moment. Each man looked very serious, and with the blacked faces their eyes looked wide open. Louis wondered if everyone felt what he was feeling, the sense of nausea as the C-47 plane lurched this way and that with each flak burst. Louis felt sweat where his skin touched his uniform, and he found himself wiping the sweat from the palm of his hands on his trousers. He felt beads of sweat running down the side of his brow and wondered if it would streak his black-face camouflage. He looked around for a moment at those fellow paratroopers sitting nearest him to see if anyone else was sweating. He simply could not tell in the darkness. But he did his best to show no fear, as did each man who also knew what Louis knew: they were all in this together and needed and depended on each man doing his duty—no matter what!

The sky now lit up like fireworks on July 4th as the flak from German anti-aircraft guns began to fill the sky. It was beautiful, Louis thought with a slight smile, thinking of the great fireworks displays back home. But this was a deadly light show. Each blast seemed closer than the last, and each time the concussion of the blast made the C-47 shudder and shake. The sound of the other C-47s in the close formation began to soften just a little as the planes tried to spread apart to avoid colliding with each other in the dense clouds they had just entered. Plus, the planes needed more room to maneuver to take evasive action to avoid the flak bursts. Some planes began to fly faster and at greater altitude than planned to also avoid the intense German flak barrage. Louis remembered what their commanding officer had said when they were preparing to board the C-47s in their final briefing: "Don't worry, men, the Germans are not expecting us, they will be sound asleep in their beds, we'll take them by surprise silently falling from the sky."

Louis laughed to himself when he remembered that comment. Well, at least a few Germans were wide awake and shooting everything they had into the sky already. And any Germans who were still in bed were awake now with all the noise and racket going on all over the French coast. Awake or not, we were coming!

Then a loud explosion rocked the C-47 hard and lifted it straight up, then down. The bounce knocked several men off their seats and onto the deck of the plane. These men had been seated directly across from Louis. He realized with the flash of light from each shell burst out in the darkness and clouds that he could now see large holes in the side of the plane. These men were not bounced out of their seats—they were blown off their seats by shrapnel from the last close blast of flak. Several of the men on the deck moaned, one tried to get to his feet, two did not move at all. The jump master moved over and began checking each man for injuries. He yelled at the top of his voice for all the men to stay put. As Louis looked down, he could see a growing pool of blood on the deck with each burst of light from an exploding flak shell. Other men sitting nearby could also see the expanding pool of blood flowing from beneath the two men who were not moving. Several men vomited onto the deck right in front of them. The smell of vomit began to mingle with the smell of fear as the reality of combat suddenly took hold of this stick of paratroopers, who found themselves in the thick of combat before they'd even left the plane.

Another close burst of flak rocked the plane again on Louis' side. It seemed to hit near the nose of the plane. Within a moment of that burst, the green jump light came on, and the plane seemed to nose over into a steep dive. Wait a minute, Louis thought, as panic flooded his mind. We are moving really fast, way too fast for jumping according to our drills in training. And, the plane is supposed to go into a climb when we jump, so we are actually walking downhill toward the open door, not struggling uphill from a plane in a steep and fast dive. But no sooner did Louis realize this when the green jump light came on and the sergeant jump-master yelled, "GO! GO! Hook up and jump—NOW!"

The men who could stand up hooked up their static lines and started struggling uphill toward the open jump door. Those closest to the door made it out fairly quickly. Other men found themselves slipping and falling onto the vomit and blood covered deck. Each man had nearly 100 pounds of gear strapped to his body, and it made it almost impossible to climb uphill on the slippery metal deck to the open jump door. Then as several men slipped on the deck and fell over, their static jump lines began to tangle. James pulled himself to his feet and held onto the static line and did a quick pivot over the pile of men struggling to get back to their feet. He reached back and extended his outstretched hand to Louis to pull him forward of the pile of men on the deck. Louis took James' hand and made it past the tangled mass of static lines and wounded men—just as he watched James dive out the jump door into the clouds and darkness. Then another blast shook the C-47 violently. It knocked Louis off his feet and back onto the pile of men on the deck, still tangled in their static lines, gear, and slipping in the vomit and blood.

Louis thought the plane had just been blown out of the sky. He instantly realized the plane could be only seconds away from crashing into the ground, if it did not explode before impact! He could see a flaming red-orange glow surrounding the plane outside the jump door. Smoke filled the cabin of the plane and made it harder to see or breathe. Within another minute Louis had crawled on his hands and knees uphill to the jump door and pulled himself out the opening head first, as he dived into the darkness. But instead of clearing the plane with a forced jump out the door, Louis was only able to slide headfirst out the opening. As he hit the rush of wind past the door moving nearly 200 mph, he was slammed violently into the back side of the jump door. He felt his leg absorb the full impact as he cleared the door. But no time to think about that now. Within an instant of clearing the plane, a massive explosion filled the sky directly over his head. It seemed the C-47 exploded just after Louis cleared the door. In that same instant Louis' parachute had burst open above his head. His first impulse was to watch overhead to make certain the explosion of the C-47 did not collapse or damage his parachute canopy. He felt a quick sense of relief that it seemed perfectly intact.

Then Louis wondered how far apart he was from his jump buddy James, who went out the C-47 just before him. Louis peered out into the clouds and darkness—he could see nothing but the constant burst of anti-aircraft shells lighting up the sky around C-47s overhead, roaring onward toward their drop zones. Okay, no sign of any other paratroopers falling from the sky. What's next? Louis wondered as he looked down. There was the ground just below him! It was coming at him so fast he had no time to prepare to hit the ground—it just came up and hit him so hard it felt like his body had been slammed against the earth!

Louis lay there for a moment, recovering from the impact and gasping for his breath that had just been knocked out of him. First thought…am I alive? Guess so, I am still thinking, and seeing and feeling—I think? Then a quick assessment of his condition. Do I hurt? Am I injured? Yes, every joint in his body ached. But nothing seemed really injured and he was not wounded. Then Louis realized the billowing silk canopy was floating directly over his head, being held aloft by a soft flowing breeze. Must bury the damn parachute, Louis thought, remembering the first order upon landing. He rolled to his feet and began to gather the parachute lines and silk canopy into him to wad the thing up into a manageable ball for burial.

As Louis did this, he also was scanning all around the area where he had landed—looking, hopefully, for other members of his unit of paratroopers. Nothing, just a big open field surrounded by hedgerow trees. Lucky landing, Louis thought; wide open place, but what a target too. Then Louis heard voices directly behind him! They were talking in German and he wheeled around toward the sound of the voices, dropped his bundled parachute, and began to unholster his M1A1 Carbine from the leg holster. It hung up in the holster and it was hard to pull out. As the carbine finally emerged from his leg holster, Louis could see in the darkness that the barrel of the rifle was bent! Somehow in jumping and the fast-hard landing, the carbine barrel was bent. The carbine was useless. Great! Louis could feel his heart pounding, his mouth was dry as cotton, his mind raced in panic—adrenalin was driving his energy and he knew he had to act now and fast!

For a moment he remembered one of their orders was to try to not fire their weapons until daylight—to preserve the element of surprise! Louis laughed to himself; too late to worry about surprising the Germans! I could not fire my weapon now if I had to! Louis, your bad luck is still with you, nothing has changed!

Again the German voices were heard by Louis and he looked up to see lights coming on in a farmhouse near the edge of the field. Three German soldiers emerged onto the front porch of the farmhouse and were shouting toward Louis as they put on their coats. It seemed to Louis, who spoke and understood German since his early childhood, that the soldiers were saying, "Hey, American paratrooper, we've been expecting you! Come here, have a cup of coffee with us…? That's so friendly sounding, Louis thought. Next thing you know they will come over here and say, "Hello, can we help you bury your parachute?"

Louis realized he was an easy target, clearly out in the open, a fluffy white parachute bundle lying at his feet, and no carbine with which to fight! He began to move as fast as he could in the opposite direction toward the hedgerow and the safety of the dense, dark cover they offered. No shots were fired, to Louis' relief, as he made it to the hedgerow and cover. Louis moved along the hedgerow in the direction away from the farmhouse. Overhead he could still hear the steady roar of C-47s, but now it seemed more distant.

So did the anti-aircraft bursts. Louis finally stopped, and breathless, rested against the dark tangle of hedge tree undergrowth. He began to assess his situation, as his heart still pounded and his mind raced, while his eyes strained to see in the darkness and misty fog, scanning in all directions around his position.

Louis thought silently to himself, well, here I am, on the ground in France, German occupied France. I am alive, alone, and without a weapon except for my bayonet. I am not injured. And, I guess I am lucky because I think I was the last man alive to leave that C-47. But if that is lucky, I could sure use a little more right now.

Then, thinking about his luck, and his life, which up to now had seemed uncommonly unlucky, Louis found himself remembering what, up until this night, had been the worst night of his life—the night his mother did not come home. He felt that same familiar and lonely fear saturate his heart and mind. The old sadness he had always known and deep pain in his chest at these thoughts crowded out his present and deadly situation. He was all alone, again.

Alex & Theresa Pfeifer, ca. 1925

Chapter 2
A farmhouse north of Hays, Kansas,
on the morning of February 18, 1926

Good-bye, Mother

"Where is Mommy?" nearly two-year-old Louis asked, standing in the doorway to the kitchen. Everyone was already up, and it seemed very early—the glow of early sunrise was just beginning to light the house. It was very quiet. No one was saying a word. Dad was just sitting at the kitchen table, holding his head in both his hands. You could not see his face, but he seemed very sad. He had bandages wrapped around his head that covered his eyes. The sheriff also sat at the table. He was just staring at Dad.

The eerie stillness in the kitchen, combined with the ice cold floor he was standing barefoot upon and the muffled howl of the incessant wind outside, made Louis shiver with cold fear.

Louis' oldest sister, Martina, who was 12 years old, was standing beside Dad; her hand was on his shoulder. Everyone else was in the room too, just standing against the walls. Louis walked over to Martina and pulled on her dress. "Where is Mommy?" She looked down at Louis and her soft brown eyes met his. They were full of tears; frightened, very sad eyes. "Jerry, take Louis into the bedroom. He should not have to see all this. And put some socks on his bare feet too,

15

honey—the floor is very cold and here he is in his bare feet," Martina said as she wiped the tears from her cheek with the back of her hand.

Jerry, Louis' other sister, who was just a year older than Louis, was watching his every move from the time he first entered the room. She always looked after Louis, and took several steps across the room and said, "Come, Louis, let's go put on some socks." As she took his hand, he looked up into her big dewy brown eyes. They always seemed to glow with an inner love and kindness, and she had the voice to match that warm, kind heart. But this morning, her eyes were also wet with tears and red from crying, and so puffy it made Louis' heart ache to look at her sad eyes.

As the two entered the boy's bedroom, Jerry picked Louis up and sat him on the bed. She wiped tears from her cheeks with the sleeve of her pajamas as she turned and walked the few steps to the dresser that held their socks. She returned with a pair of thick cotton socks that had been darned many times over in the heel and toes as "hand-me-downs" from their three older brothers. Jerry knelt down on both knees in front of Louis as he sat on the bed. She rolled up one sock, then another, and slid them up on his bare feet.

"Jerry, where is Mommy? And, why is Sheriff Weltz here? Why is Daddy so sad?" Jerry did not answer as she continued to put on both of Louis' socks. Then she looked up at his eyes and reached up to hold his face with both her hands. She gently held his face with a hand on each cheek and looked straight into his eyes with her dark brown, but teary, red puffy eyes and said, "Louis, Daddy came home this morning very early, but Mommy did not come home with him."

"But, where is Mommy?" Louis asked again, in a hushed whisper, as he felt a growing panic that something terrible must be wrong, because she should be here, she was always here. Then the sound of heavy footsteps on the back porch made his heart leap with joy! It must be Mommy at last! Louis jumped down from the bed and ran into the kitchen doorway yelling, "Mommy!" at just the moment the kitchen door opened. The room was instantly flooded with frigid cold air and the bright glare of sunlight as the sun was just clearing the horizon. For a moment Louis was blinded by the brightness of the sunlight. Then as his eyes recovered he felt the cold, frigid air embrace him and all those standing around the kitchen. Shivering, he could see a large man enter the kitchen through the open door. At first he could only see the silhouette against the bright sunlight. This seemed very odd—it was not his mother as Louis expected, but a large man carrying something, no, someone... yes, a small woman was in his arms—that must be... "Mother!" Louis cried out as he rushed across the kitchen to embrace his mother's body. He was caught from behind by Jerry, his sister, who swept little Louis up in her arms and turned him around in a big hug, as strong as she could hold him, now facing the other direction, away from the scene unfolding in the kitchen.

But Louis was also strong and would not be denied the awareness of what was happening. He squirmed his way around in his sister's arms and saw the large man walk across the floor of the kitchen to the big dinner table. He gently laid the stiff, frozen body of Theresa, his mother, down on the kitchen table on her side. Louis saw that she was frozen stiff, her eyes were still open, now looking straight at Jerry and him in each other's arms. But her eyes did not glow with the warm twinkle of love and recognition they expected to see. No, her eyes were still, motionless, lifeless. He could see she was not anything like their mother. She was stiff, unmoving, unbreathing, unnatural....

Louis turned his eyes from her with horror as the realization that was gripping his mind became undeniable. She was frozen. Mother was dead. Then he could feel Jerry's chest begin to heave and quake with sobs as she also realized their mother was dead. Louis felt a lonely fear come over him. He knew that somehow this changed everything, that his short life, as he had known it, was now over, just as his mother's life was now over. All that part of him was gone now, gone with her, his warm, loving mother. Whatever remained, whatever was to follow, would never be the same.... This new, great unknown filled Louis with dread as he squeezed his arms even tighter around his sister's neck, and held on very tight, and she too held him very close. Jerry was all Louis had now, the one person he knew really loved him.

Aunt Maria, their mother's sister, who had married Uncle Adam, their father's brother, had been called very early by Alex, the children's father, seeking help. They had both rushed over as quickly as they could given the extreme severity of the blizzard the night before. Aunt Maria took a kettle of warm water from the stove and, with tears running down her cheeks, she poured hot water into a basin. She dipped a towel into the warm water and rung it out. Then she gently placed the warm, wet, steaming towel over her sister Theresa's frigid, frozen eyes. All of Theresa's six children were watching Aunt Maria's every move as she cleared the snow and ice from the dead and frozen stiff body of their mother. After a moment, she pulled the towel away and gently pressed her sister Theresa's eyelids down over her soft brown eyes. Those eyes were staring directly at Louis and Jerry as she lay on the kitchen table. Steam was beginning to rise from her clothing as the warmth of the kitchen penetrated her frozen mass. In that instant, as her eyelids were closed by Aunt Maria, Louis took one quick last look into his mother's eyes—her eyes once so full of love and life, and in his heart, yes, deep within his heart Louis was certain he saw her love light still reaching out to him and Jerry. The last images she would reflect back from those soft brown eyes, yet still love seemed to radiate out from those now staring eyes. Yes, from deep within her frozen, lifeless body, love still seemed to glow to Louis and Jerry from those now still eyes.

Louis' second oldest brother, Fred, had been standing in the far corner of the room. Along with Marcel, the next oldest, and Gene, the oldest brother, they watched their first born sister, Martina, offer to help Aunt Maria. Fred spoke in a soft voice but was heard by all in the silence of the room: "Mom's the color of a rose, a pink rose—she is so beautiful...." Louis and Jerry, and all the others, looked over to Fred as he spoke, and tears left his swollen eyes as he stood there looking at his mother's lifeless form. Marcel was quiet, but also crying. Gene, older, taller, and mature for his years, remained strong. He had already learned there was no profit in showing your feelings, especially around his dad.

Aunt Maria continued to use the warm water and towel to clean the ice and frozen snow from Theresa's nose, her ears, and her mouth. Tears still streaming down her face, she worked her way down to her frozen sister's hands. After a few moments with warm towels pressed to her frozen stiff arms and hands, it was becoming possible to move them. One hand was pressed tightly against her chest and the other outstretched, her entire arm extended straight up, as if reaching for help from heaven. Finally, after several moments of warmth, Aunt Maria began to open her sister's outstretched hand enough to remove the leather gloves she wore. "Oh no! No, no, no…" Aunt Maria sighed as she saw her sister's palms. Her moaning sigh caught everyone's attention in the kitchen as they saw what she was so upset about. Even Louis could see, and understood why—why his mother's hands were sliced to the bone, sliced open over and over again. Ripped to shreds until her leather gloves were virtually without palms. To keep from being lost in that hellish blizzard, she was walking and crawling in the deep snowdrifts, hanging on to the barbed wire fences. She had pulled herself along the razor sharp barbed wire, slicing her hands open over and over again.

"She was found under the barbed wire fence just east of the house," Sheriff Weltz said. "She was only about 100 yards from the house. That close. She was nearly buried in the snow which had drifted up to the second strand of wire in that area. Even higher in many spots. The only reason we found her was that her one arm was still extended, reaching up, and with her gloved hand she gripped the top strand of wire, as if she could not, or would not, let go—not give up. That is all we saw, a gloved hand reaching up out of the snowdrift under a barbed wire fence, holding on for dear life. For dear, sweet life."

"We had to dig her out. She was frozen to the wet ground under the snow. What a hell of a night. Damn blizzard!" Doctor Betthauser sighed under his breath.

Dr. Samuel Betthauser was the family doctor. He led the search party that had arrived by horse and wagon very early that morning, before sun up. Dr. Betthauser, along with Dr. Wisdom, the town undertaker and coroner, had found Louis' mother, Mrs. Theresa Pfeifer.

Sheriff Weltz, who had been sitting in a chair at the table opposite Alex Pfeifer, Theresa's husband, and father of their six children, said nothing. But he never took his eyes off of Alex as he stood up slowly. He was tall, lean, and solidly built, with grey hair curled thinly from under his wide brimmed Stetson. He took his gaze from Alex and slowly looked around the room, first to Martina, still standing beside her father with her hand on his shoulder. Then over to the three boys, standing in the corner nearest to the stove, then to the doorway to the boy's room, where Jerry stood, still holding Louis in her arms, with her back sagging down from Louis' weight. And finally down to Theresa's frozen corpse lying on her side on the kitchen table. Still locked in the semi-fetal position as she was found. Sheriff Weltz again looked over to Jerry, the second youngest, and Louis, the youngest, in her arms. He walked over to them and knelt down on one knee, gently taking Louis into his outreaching arms, and relieving Jerry of the burden she had been holding with so much love. He put Louis on his knee, then pulled Jerry over to him too, and in a voice so low and quiet it was barely heard by anyone else in the room, he said, "Your mom has joined God in heaven, along with all the angels and saints, but I am sure she is also still here, watching over you, and loving you two, just like always... now, you two be strong and brave, your sister and brothers will need your help, and so will your dad too. And I promise you, I will find out exactly what happened to your mother, and why she did not make it home last night with your dad." Weltz then eased Louis off his bended knee and onto the floor. Jerry was still holding Louis' hand. Sheriff Weltz stood up, tall, straight, and looked back down into each of their eyes and smiled a warm but slight smile. Then he winked and turned around. Facing the others in the room, and taking another glance at Alex, who had never looked up, and still cradling his bandaged head in his hands, Weltz said, "I need some air." He walked across the kitchen floor and out the door onto the side porch.

As Weltz opened his coat and reached inside to his shirt pocket for his cigarettes, Dr. Betthauser came out the door and joined him on the porch. Weltz offered Betthauser a cigarette, who declined, as Weltz lit his smoke with his

Zippo. Dr. Betthauser slowly shook his head no, saying, "Not sure those damn things do you any good, Weltz." They stood there in silence for a while, each with his own thoughts, surveying the snow-swept fields. The sun was low in the morning sky to the east, a harsh chilling wind was still blowing from the north, and the glare of the snow-covered fields made your eyes ache, yet it was beautiful too—surreal, a frozen sea of white waves of drifted snow; that and nothing more could be seen in all directions.

"Just how does a man get separated from his wife in a blizzard, leaves her behind, at the mercy of the elements?" Sheriff Weltz wondered out loud.

"She was not the only one left behind," Dr. Betthauser answered. Sheriff Weltz slowly turned his head toward Dr. Betthauser, inviting an explanation of that comment. As their eyes met, a glint of understanding was absorbed in Sheriff Weltz's mind. Dr. Betthauser said, "That's right, she was pregnant. She was not exactly on her own, she had a child within her, so she also had to worry about its survival too." Dr. Betthauser could see a mist of moisture well up in Sheriff Weltz's eyes, and the redness of sadness filled the whites of his eyes. "How long...?"

"About three months. Yes, Alex knew. Not sure he was too thrilled with another mouth to feed, times being so tough and all, but what do I know about that?"

Weltz took a long draw on his cigarette and slowly let his breath fill the air. The smoke merged with the steam of his breath around his face for a brief moment. "Well, Doc, only one person knows how this happened, and if you think he is fit to travel, I would like to take him into town to get his story straight."

"I checked him out when I first got here. He is severely frostbitten on his face, fingers, and toes. His vision will be blurred for quite some time, snow blindness at that degree does not clear up overnight. He may well have permanent damage to his eyes. I am more worried about his lungs breathing the frigid air all those hours. He is likely to go into pneumonia. But, in time he should be all right. Yet physically, given the hell he and his wife must have gone through last night, I expect he feels pretty rough. So, do not be too hard on him, Sheriff. He has had a big shock, plus survived one hellish ordeal," Dr. Betthauser said. Their attention was turned to the snow-drifted road as a funeral wagon drawn by a team of two horses turned into the lane toward the house. It was driven by the coroner's assistant and carrying Father Grotz, of St. Joseph Catholic Church, Sister Mary Margaret, and Cecelia Pfeifer—Alex's mother and the children's grandmother.

"Looks like the coroner is ready to take the deceased Mrs. Pfeifer back to town," Dr. Betthauser observed as he turned to go inside the farmhouse and the warmth of the kitchen. Sheriff Weltz flipped his cigarette away and followed Dr. Betthauser into the house.

"As soon as Father Grotz has said last rites, they can be on their way. I will ask Alex to come with me to my office for more treatment, and then you can come over to my office for your interview. I will be your witness and take notes for you. Okay with you?" Dr. Betthauser asked Sheriff

Weltz, who only nodded his head yes, in agreement.

"Sister Mary Margaret can stay and help Grandma Pfeifer take care of the children until we sort all this out," Sheriff Weltz said as he opened the front door and helped the new arrivals out of the wagon and into the house.

Chapter 3

After the jump into hell

As Louis moved along the hedgerow, away from the Germans in the farmhouse, he felt like a hunted jackrabbit must feel when the hunter comes to the field to shoot them. He had been one of those hunters when he was younger—ready and anxious to shoot any jackrabbit that moved across his field of view. Now he understood how the jackrabbit must feel. At any moment a bullet out of no-where, with no warning, could end his life—or wound him so severely that he might wish he were dead. Louis felt his heart pounding like a big drum within his chest.

Then he heard a noise just ahead. He stopped. Frozen in absolute stillness. He peered into the darkness and foggy mist in the direction of the noise dead ahead along the hedge-row. Nothing. No sound. No movement, only coal black shadows and misty darkness. Louis very slowly reached into his pocket to retrieve the little metal cricket he was given to signal a fellow paratrooper. As he began to pinch it be-tween his thumb and forefinger, he also realized this sudden "click—click" would give up his position and identity too as an American paratrooper. Plus, in training some of the fellas joked that the first thing the Germans would do when they captured or killed any of us would be to retrieve these little crickets and start stalking the woods going "Click—click, come out, stupid American paratroopers…."

There was a long silence. Louis strained his eyes and ears toward the darkness just ahead in the hedgerow. He held his cricket in his fingers, but kept it silent. Then he heard the "click—click" of another cricket dead ahead of his position, just about ten paces away! He waited a moment, and then said the password in a quiet whisper: "FLASH!" A long instant passed, then a voice Louis knew and was glad to hear said, "THUNDER! Louis! Is that you?" The same familiar voice whispered, "It's me, James! James, James." Louis felt a rush of relief soak his body, and realized he was already wet with sweat, and his joints and muscles ached from the tension. "James! What took you so long to use that damn cricket? I might have shot you if my rifle did not have a bent barrel! Or at least a bayonet charge…," laughing as he moved forward to embrace James, his buddy.

"Did anyone else make it out of our plane besides you, Louis?" James asked.

"No, I was the last one out and it blew up just as I cleared the door. I would never have gotten out without your help, buddy," Louis replied. "Damn mess. Lucky to be alive."

"Yes, we both are, so far…," James said. "Any idea exactly where we are…?"

"Hell no—nothing looks familiar or like it is supposed to based on those sand terrain boards we were briefed on," Louis replied with exasperation and his usual ironic grin.

"Maybe after daylight we can pick up a landmark, or a road sign, or something. But with Germans crawling all over the place hunting us, we better keep low and not make any light trying to study the map. Let's just move out and try to find more of our unit."

"Right," James answered. "I did see only one guy from our unit, could not tell who he was in the mist, but he landed on a concrete dragon tooth. He was bent over backwards and crying for his mother. I think his back was broken. I began to climb up to help him and the bullets began to fly. He was shot dead. At least that put him out of his misery," James said. Even in the dark Louis could see tears welling up in James' eyes. "Is that the first time…?" Louis asked. "Yeah man, first combat death I saw…brutal too, man! They just missed me and I got the hell out of there and took cover. So, I know we do not want to go in the direction I just came from," James said.

"Jeez," Louis said in a soft whisper, "We cannot go back where I came from either, and Germans are surely hunting me now after they watched me land from a farmhouse porch, just beyond the other field."

"Look, let's take our chances on the road just beyond the next hedgerow. Maybe we can make better time and pick up some other guys too. We can always dive for cover if we are seen," James suggested.

"Right," Louis agreed.

The two walked all day the following day. Never saw a single German or American. They were just way too far inland from their drop zone. They kept close to the hedgerows and kept their heads down. With no sleep at all the first night, and very little sleep the second night, they were both exhausted. Plus there was small arms fire constantly coming from all directions around them. But the rush of adrenalin filled them with a weary alertness, knowing that sudden death lurked in every shadow and around each bend in their path.

They stopped for a break and took refuge in deep cover along a hedgerow. The two men were quiet for a long time. Then James said, "Louis, I have been thinking a lot about our flight. All that flak and turbulence. Remember how the plane took on more speed and then our formation began to break up?"

"Yeah, we turned this way, and then that . . . it seemed like we were bouncing all over the sky!"

"Well, by my estimates, if our plane was only going 180 miles per hour…then that is three miles per minute air speed. Okay? Say it took us just two extra minutes to clear the door and jump…and if we were directly over our drop zone when the green light came on…well, in just two minutes at three miles per minute…hell, Louis, we could have missed our drop zone by six miles—or more! No wonder we cannot find anyone else from our unit!"

Louis did not say anything, but he was amused at how smart James was, always thinking and analyzing everything. Perhaps if my life had not been so chaotic, I would be as smart as James in math and such things too, Louis thought to himself as he scanned the fields and trees that lined them to the horizon for any sign of friendly, or not friendly, troopers.

Late that second night James asked, "Louis, don't you

wish we were back in Alliance, Nebraska? We could tell those jump instructors a few more things about jumping into combat now than they told us. Right? Remember that cold, snowy night we went to the movies? We had a pint of whiskey and shared it during the movie. As soon as we got outside, standing there in our warm overcoats on the sidewalk, you just passed out and fell over face first on the pavement! I remember I thought you were just cutting up... until you just lay there!" James chuckled quietly to himself.

"Broke my damn nose!" Louis said with another ironic grin. "I was unconscious for a long time too. About three days later our company was going on a long hike into the hills, and my nose was still hurting like hell. So I told myself it was a good time to take my nose to see the base doctor. He took a long look at my swollen nose and asked, "When did this happen?" I answered, "Oh, two or three days ago, Doc."

"Well it is too late to do anything about it now, it has already started growing back," the doc said.

"Don't worry, Louis, that big schnoz makes you look tough now, like a prize fighter or a gangster. You will get lots of respect from the Germans with that big nose too, no doubt about it," James added.

"Yeah, that is what I'm afraid of, plus no respect from the ladies either," Louis said with another ironic grin.

He remembered silently to himself that he had sent his sister Jerry a picture of himself taken just after he broke his nose. She wrote back and said he looked like a thug or gangster now. Louis smiled at the thought of his sister. In many ways she was all he had, and all he'd ever had. The one person he knew he could always count on. He wondered what she was doing at that moment in time back in Kansas City.

That pleasant thought was soon overshadowed by the return of that uncertain feeling of fear, knowing that death at any moment was the present reality. He could not keep his mind from returning to another time when uncertainty and fear were all he had in his life.

Chapter 4

A helluva night

Dr. Betthauser had finished checking out Alex Pfeifer. He was in critical condition given the ordeal he had just endured. The approximately six hours spent wandering in a frigid blizzard had left him with frostbitten fingers and toes, which should heal without permanent damage. But his face was very frostbitten and that would bear close watching and medication. Most serious was his eyes. He was clearly snow-blinded. There might be permanent damage to his eyes. The time spent trying to look directly into the wind-driven snow to see his way had lacerated the eye tissues severely. But his lungs had breathed frigid air for too many hours and he was going into pneumonia. "Only time will tell how this will heal," Dr. Betthauser explained to Sheriff Weltz.

"Okay," Weltz said, "but is he well enough to give me his statement so I can go back to my office?"

"He has been through a lot, Sheriff, so take it easy and let's give it a go," Dr. Betthauser replied.

"Alex, I need for you to tell me what happened to you and your wife this past night. Dr. Betthauser is here too and he is going to take some notes for me, okay?"

Alex nodded slowly. His eyes were heavily bandaged and he saw only total darkness. But even as the first question was asked, his mind began to replay the events of the previous evening.

He and his wife, Theresa, planned on going to Hays for Ash Wednesday Mass. They were leaving the children home because the youngest, Louis, was sick. The two older kids, Gene, 11, and Martina, 12, could watch the kids just fine. They would pick up some medicine for Louis before the Mass, and then afterwards perhaps drop in for a visit with Grandma Cecelia Pfeifer, Alex's mother, who lived in town.

As they started out, a steady and heavy rain was still coming down. It had been raining all afternoon. A good and welcome rain for all the wheat farmers in the county, including Alex. This much moisture in the ground this early would help get the crop out of the ground in early spring. And the rain would settle all the dust from the frequent dust storms of recent weeks.

The two set out in the 1922 Model T Ford touring car, dressed for church in their Sunday best, and with only canvas side curtains to keep the weather out. They had no way of knowing the weather was about to take such a dramatic turn for the worst. During Mass, just after 7:00 P.M., the rain began to change to snow. The winds picked up and blew strong directly out of the north. The temperature began to fall rapidly. The snow covered the wet ground quickly and soon was blowing into drifts of rising white waves, growing deeper with each passing minute.

When Alex and Theresa emerged from Mass with the rest of the congregation, they were greeted with a strong blast of frigid wind driving flakes of snow the size of quarters to half dollars. The snow was already several inches deep and drifts were beginning to form very fast. Alex and Theresa were well aware of the rapid changes in weather in the region. Both had spent all their lives in the Hays area and the surrounding Ellis County, Kansas.

"We will make a short stop at Mom's house, and then head home before this gets any worse," Alex said to Theresa. Theresa was pregnant and already felt a little queasy; now the added worry of getting home and her concern for the six children at home made her feel ill.

"Alex, maybe we should just go directly home?"

"We will be just fine," Alex replied as he drove off down Walnut Street from St. Joseph Catholic Church toward the north edge of town and Grandma Pfeifer's home. When they arrived, the road was already covered with 3 to 4 inches of snow and drifts up to 12 inches were forming around buildings. Grandma Pfeifer welcomed them. She gave them a hot toddy and urged them to consider spending the night at her home.

Grandma Cecelia Pfeifer lived in a large white bungalow on the corner. She had bought the entire block of lots when she retired from the farm. She would sell off a lot occasionally to support herself. Her husband, Alex's father, Johannes Adam Pfeifer, had immigrated to the United States from Herzog, Russia, in 1878. He became a very successful and wealthy farmer. He was able to leave a large acreage farm to each of his children when he passed away in 1917 at only 58 years of age.

"The kids will be all right. They have plenty of food and

fuel to keep warm, right?" Cecelia asked Alex, who nodded in agreement as he sipped his hot toddy.

"Louis needs his medicine and we need to be there," Theresa answered in a sharp tone of finality, which made it clear to all that she had only one intention, and that was to return home to her children as soon as possible. Theresa did not drink her hot toddy. Not good for the baby inside her, and she already felt too ill.

"Want some hot tea, dear?" Grandma Pfeifer asked her as she picked up the untouched hot toddy and set it down beside Alex to finish.

"No, Grandma, do not bother. I think we just need to go," Theresa replied with the same final tone. Within a few minutes Alex, after downing his second hot toddy, and Theresa were underway again in the Ford Model T touring car.

As they passed north out of town and onto the open road, the going got much more difficult to continue. The rain-soaked mud roads, now covered with about six inches of snow, were very slippery. It was getting more and more difficult to get traction, and the regular drifts of 12 to 18 inches of snow made matters worst. Finally they were reaching the last seven hills before they were home. This stretch of road was the last one and one-half miles before home. But it was also the worst. There were seven hills, each one steeper than the last and rising farther than the last as they climbed to the higher ground north of Hays. Their farm home set on a high hill overlooking Hays and Ellis County to the south.

Alex decided to stop again, before beginning the climb

up the seven hills, at the last neighbor's house before their own home. In spite of the late hour—it was now past 9:00 P.M.—they were welcomed. Hot drinks were offered again, which Alex accepted and Theresa declined. A discussion of the weather conditions ensued. The neighbors urged them to spend the night, and again Theresa declined the invitation. Her strong motherly instincts demanded her prompt return home to her children. Alex borrowed some fuel to be certain he had enough to complete the trip, just in case the going got rougher than it already had been. Soon, they set off again. Now past 11:00 P.M., on a drive that under normal conditions would take less than twenty minutes.

One by one they climbed each of the seven hills. It was a continuous struggle against nature, wind, and gravity. The mud and snow cover on the dirt road made for almost no traction. The drifts in some cases made it nearly impossible to continue. Several times on each hill, Alex got out to clear snow with his feet and tried to open a path in the snow for the wheels to negotiate. He was not dressed for this kind of frigid weather, nor was Theresa.

Theresa sat on the passenger side fighting the fear rising inside her. She was worried about the children. She was more worried about herself and Alex and their Model T. What if they could not make it? What if they got stuck, or ran off the road, or the Model T just froze up . . . or ran out of gas? A constant flood of worries filled her mind. Plus the frigid temperatures were slowly penetrating her clothing, and the chill made her teeth begin to rattle uncontrollably.

Finally, after an undetermined time they cleared the last

hill. Home had to be less than one mile away. But in the pitch black night, they could see nothing but wind-driven snow directly in front of them. The snow was so intense that white-out conditions made it impossible to see more than a few feet ahead. Alex was also feeling the frigid and penetrating cold. His frequent trips out of the Model T to clear a snow path for the wheels had made his shoes, socks, and slacks wet with snow. His feet were starting to feel numb.

Just then a sudden and strong gush of wind pushed the Model T to the right! Alex steered against the wind as the wheels plowed into a snowdrift about thirty-six inches high and pulled the Model T hard to the right and into the deep ditch along the side of the road. The Model T came to a sudden lurching stop against the bank of the ditch. Alex was thrown hard to the right directly on top of Theresa, who was also thrown hard to the right against the inside of the Model T.

They both sat there for a moment, stunned with the sudden and jarring stop. Alex began to pull himself back off Theresa and asked her if she was all right. Theresa did not answer for a long moment. She was hurting from the lurch to the right, then being hit hard by Alex sliding suddenly against her with his full body weight.

"Now what?" she said to Alex, not mentioning the pain she was feeling, nor the growing numbness from the frigid cold.

Alex tried to help her find a more comfortable position. The Model T was now sitting at a steep slope to the right. The only way out was to climb across the front seat and crawl out the driver side. The engine was dead and the cold began to penetrate them from all directions, driven by the unrelenting wind and snow.

Alex crawled out of the car. He stomped around the entire car. It was not easy. In some places the snow had drifted to over three feet deep. It was waist deep in the ditch, and a sticky mud base made it very hard to walk without losing your shoes as the mud tried to suck them off your feet. The motor stalled and it could not be started due to the crank being too low to the road.

Alex returned to the driver side and told Theresa there was no hope of getting the Model T out of the ditch. They would have to make for the house on foot. He helped Theresa pull herself out of the driver's side of the Model T. The minute she felt the full force of the frigid wind, her head began a pounding pain, a throbbing ache that instantly felt unbearable. Yet, she and Alex must endure this and move as quickly as they could toward the house.

Alex, already feeling the same headache pain from the frigid wind, surveyed their location. They had made it to the last hilltop. The house had to be directly to the west and slightly to the north across the field. Perhaps just less than a mile. The other option would be to walk north along the road about one mile, then west along the road perhaps just under a mile to the driveway. But then another 100 yards to the house, which was set far off the road. It only took a moment for Alex to rationalize that under these conditions, the shortest route to their home was the only chance to survive. But visibility was perhaps less than twenty feet.

A growing sense of terror and peril began to rise inside of each of them.

They crossed the road, through the ditch on the west side, to the barbed wire fence. Alex helped Theresa step through the fence. A very difficult maneuver in a full dress, and naturally it ripped as it hung up on the wire.

"We are going straight across this field to the wire fence on the other side. Then just a short distance north along the fence and we should be able to see the house," Alex yelled to Theresa, who given the howling of the wind in her ear could barely comprehend what he was saying. She just nodded in agreement.

As they walked west into the wind, each step took extraordinary effort. The visibility was nearly zero and you could not look ahead anyway because the wind-driven snow felt like ice razors slicing your face and eyes. So both moved in slow, deliberate steps with their heads down to protect them from the wind. They tried to walk straight west. They needed to walk directly west to reach the other side and the fence, then north to the house.

But with each step the wind drove them a little to the south, away from their destination. After perhaps an hour, they had only crossed a field about a half mile wide. They did reach the other side—the barbed wire fence told them so. But they were both totally exhausted and the penetrating cold and head pain was unbearable. The effects of hypothermia were clearly setting in, and both wanted to stop and rest. Perhaps to sleep only for a moment or two. Neither could speak without very focused concentration, and both were shivering uncontrollably.

"I…want…to stop, Alex, I…need…to rest…," Theresa whispered to Alex through the shivering and chatter of her teeth. Alex understood her exhaustion; he felt it too. He wanted to stop as well. To just lie down and rest, to sleep—maybe forever—but it was hard if not impossible to comprehend the consequences of stopping. They both were in the confused and growingly irrational state brought on by hypothermia.

"We made it to the fence, Theresa, the house is only a little farther, we are going to make it, we must keep going…," Alex said as he helped Theresa to her feet, picked her up in his arms, and they set off again, moving to their right along the fence, which should have taken them north and nearer to the house. Yet, it was too much for Alex, and he fell with Theresa in his arms. Picked her up again, and with great effort continued on a few more steps and fell again as they reached a snowdrift as high as the fence, making it difficult to tell just where the fence was! This was their only landmark, and they could not drift away from the fence line.

They now had no sense of time or distance covered. Only moment by moment, second by second, effort and the sheer will to live kept them both going. Then, the horror of the night. They came to a corner in the fence line! In the pitch darkness, Alex had no sense of direction. Which corner was this? Had they wandered too far north and then backtracked toward the east? Was this the northeast corner of the field? The furthest point away from the house? Or had they drifted south and made it to the south fence line of the field, which would make this the southwest corner of the field? Alex's brain ached as he tried to reason and search for answers. He wondered for a moment if it even mattered. How much longer could either of them survive in this hellish night of frigid cold, ice razor snow driven by a wind from hell?

He had to make a choice and make it now. Time was not on their side. He reasoned they had veered too far north and reached the northwest corner of the field and by turning to the left, they could head south and soon be within reach of the house. He was dead wrong. They were at the southwest corner of the field, and by going left they were now moving directly away from the house and safety. And so it went for several more hours. Constant confusion. Growing desperation. And disorientation in the total darkness of hellish cold, high winds, and heavy snow.

They were each wearing shoes for Sunday dress. Neither had expected this sudden turn in the weather nor certainly expected to be walking in deep snow. Their feet were already growing numb while they drove along in the Model T Ford. Now the pain of frostbitten feet was making each step more excruciating than the last.

Eventually Theresa and Alex could simply go no further. Her gloved hands were ripped to shreds trying to hold onto the barbed wire as they pulled themselves along the fence line. Alex's gloved hands were tougher, but still deeply cut. But it did not matter. They were already nearly frozen and neither could feel the torn flesh. She fell to the ground.

Exhausted. Weak. No strength to continue. She did not speak for a moment while Alex trudged on, unaware she had stopped. Soon, some sense overtook Alex and he realized Theresa was no longer behind him. He turned and worked his way backward along the fence. He found her lying in the snow, almost completely covered with snow. He knelt down beside her. Brushed the snow away. She said nothing. Then he bent over and slipped his hands and arms under her. He tried to pick her up to carry her, but he fell over and landed on top of her. He did not have the strength left to carry Theresa. They lay there together. Silently, the snow began to cover them both. Exhausted. Weak. They had no strength left to continue. Now, perhaps in the darkness, the frigid cold, and the howling wind, they would surrender to the never-ending sleep.

"Save yourself."

"Save the children."

"Alex, go on without me, please—think of the children."

Finally the words penetrated Alex's exhausted mind. Theresa was whispering in his ear with the only strength she had left. She was asking him to find the strength to continue onward and save himself for the children's sake, if not her own.

Alex mustered his strength. He said in a whisper in her ear, "I will go on now and come back for you. I will get help. You will be all right. Do not worry. Do not be afraid. I love you. I will come back for you. I love you."

Alex stood up. He took hold of the barbed wire fence and began to pull himself in the opposite direction from which they had come. As fate would dictate, this time he chose wisely and soon he crossed the threshold into the warmth of his own home.

Exhausted, blinded, weak, and nearly frozen, Alex first called his neighbor across the road. They woke up and took his call. It was about 3:00 A.M. He quickly told them about his long ordeal and begged for their help to come out and find Theresa. They declined and said no one could survive long outside under those conditions. Alex said no matter—he was going back out to find Theresa, his wife. And he did return into the nightmare of the hellish blizzard to search for Theresa....

Fearing loss of both Alex and Theresa, the neighbor, Mr. Walter, courageously did take off after Alex and soon found him in the same field he had wandered all night long with Theresa. When he caught up with Alex, he was now in a totally helpless state, weakened, unable to move, snow-blind, frost-bitten hands, feet, and face—plus he was totally disoriented. If he had not been found within a few more minutes, he too would not have survived the horrific blizzard conditions. Mr. Walter got Alex back into the Pfeifer home, and he called the sheriff's office to plea for help.

Several hours later, in the frigid early light of dawn, they also found Theresa. She was frozen dead. Her body was covered with deep drifted snow and lying under the same fence where she was left when Alex went on at her request. She had one hand reaching up and holding onto the top strand of barbed wire. That hand was the only thing visible, and that was how they were able to find her.

Mr. Walter, one of the neighbors who found Theresa Pfeifer, took a pink ribbon from her hair and tied it to the top wire of the fence to mark the spot where she fell and was found. That pink ribbon remained there for many years thereafter.

Chapter 5

Guest of the Third Reich

The next day Louis and James continued their march back toward their objective drop zone, as best as they could tell the direction to move. They saw a glider that had come in too fast to land and crashed. It looked so flimsy—just made of cardboard and canvas. Bodies, guns, and equipment were lying all over the field as the glider had crash-landed and just disintegrated. No survivors, that was for sure.

In another field they saw many open parachutes attached to containers that were dropped to supply paratroopers already on the ground. There were bodies of dead paratroopers who had entered the field trying to retrieve the supplies. Louis and James needed some things, but not bad enough to die for them. Plus, they were warned about booby traps, and they knew there had to be German machine gun nests overlooking the field, just waiting for anyone dumb enough to come out into the open and try to get to those containers. They just kept their heads down and continued moving out.

The sound of continuous small arms fire was all around them, from all directions. They passed many fields that had been flooded. Some had parachutes lying on the water. No doubt many of our men landed and drowned in those fields. A paratrooper was wearing about 100 pounds of gear strapped securely to his body, and a water landing would have been damned tough to survive. They were not warned about flooded fields and wondered why the intelligence gathered prior to the invasion did not pick this up. The Germans had to know we were coming and they had plenty of time to get ready for us—that was very clear, Louis and James agreed.

About mid-afternoon Louis and James came upon a series of German foxholes. They were very neat and well built. Obviously the Germans had been in France about five years and had plenty of time to prepare well-engineered fortifications. They slowly worked their way across the foxholes and found them to be abandoned. As they surveyed their perimeter, while standing on a step in the foxhole that just allowed only their eyes to be above the ground, being very quiet and very careful, they saw a group of Germans across the field that had just captured some of their guys, including their sergeant, George Leidenheimer.

The noise from small arms fire continued all around them. They whispered to each other and considered what to do next. Then suddenly they heard Germans yelling, "Hande hoch! Hande hoch!"—German for "Hands high." Louis and James turned and saw about 20 German soldiers had sneaked up on them from behind. They did not hear a thing due to all the loud weapon fire all around them. And their attention was so focused on the Germans across the field capturing some other men in their outfit.

The first impression Louis had of these German

soldiers, who now had captured him and James, was how very young they were. Louis was only 20 years old, and they were clearly much younger. They also seemed very nervous. Louis was not so nervous, no time to be scared, things were just happening too fast to be scared. They ordered Louis and James out of the trench. These young Germans were all armed with German burp guns, as they were called then—small sub-machine guns noted for having a "hair-trigger"... great! Nervous Hitler youths holding us prisoner with guns that can fire if you as much as burp, or even hiccup, Louis thought to himself. Louis could speak German and understood some of what they were saying to each other. They were actually afraid of James and him! Even though they had the two paratroopers outnumbered ten to one. As they finally climbed out of the trench and stood up with their hands up in the air, the circle of young German soldiers actually stepped back in fear and amazement. This was obviously their first encounter with the legendary 82nd Airborne paratroopers.

The German soldiers began to slowly walk around Louis and James, and told them to stick their guns into the ground barrel first. Louis still had the bayonet fixed to the barrel since that was really the only effective weapon he had. The Germans looked the two paratroopers over very closely. Maybe they were worried about booby traps too. Then one slightly older soldier approached Louis. He looked straight at Louis as he drew his combat knife from his belt. But unlike the very young German soldiers, this older sergeant showed no hint of fear in his eyes. His eyes were clear blue and hard, not even blinking. He had the look of a man who had seen death many times and grown hard by the brutal reality of war. Death now had little meaning to him, Louis thought. Louis felt absolute fear of sudden death, but kept his composure and a poker face, showing no emotion—a trait he had learned observing his own father as he grew up.

This is it, Louis thought. He may be planning on cutting my throat! Hand-to-hand combat to save your own life was no joke…but with twenty more to deal with… Hopeless? As such thoughts raced through Louis' head, the German with the knife drawn walked all around him very slowly. Louis stood very still and just kept his eye on the tip of the knife, waiting for the first thrust to make his move to defend himself…to live or die.

Then, slowly and deliberately, this soldier cut every single strap and piece of equipment Louis and James were wearing and let it fall to the ground. When he was done, they were standing there with barely anything on their bodies and with their hands up in the air. Then the rest of the soldiers got a little braver once the two paratroopers were stripped of their weapons and gear. They fell upon the gear now lying on the ground and began to search it with the desperation only starving soldiers could understand. They opened all the rations and immediately began to eat ravenously. Then they really got happy! They found the chocolate. Boy do they love chocolate. Louis heard one say in German, "If you had a chocolate bar and a bar of soap to trade, you could walk out of Germany a free man." Another added, "Plus a pack of cigarettes!" Several laughed as the chocolate bars were also consumed.

Then they found Louis' carton of Lucky Strike cigarettes. That hurt the most. They took that too, naturally. But, to his amazement, the older German soldier with the sharp knife retrieved two packs of Luckys from the others and walked over to Louis and held out his hand, holding the two packs of Luckys. He was offering to return to Louis at least two packs of his cigarettes! Louis felt a rush of relief. We had been captured all right, but at least these soldiers were not the type who shot prisoners on sight and just moved on.

Next, they marched Louis and James, along with their sergeant and the others just captured, down the road about one mile to a large barn full of other POWs. Louis knew many of them, including one of their lieutenants. Many were injured. They stayed in that building all night with no food or water from the Germans who guarded them. Most of them had not eaten since the day they'd left England.

The next day the Germans marched this entire group of POWs to Cherbourg, which was one of the prime objectives of the Allied Invasion due to a very deep harbor.

Most Germans spoke good English. They learned it in school growing up. So, you had to watch what you said around them. A German SS officer came over to interrogate the captured paratroopers one by one. He was wearing a black uniform with a golden braid on it—and he spoke excellent English. When he came to Louis and saw his name stenciled above his shirt pocket, he tapped him on the shoulder and said "Pfeifer, Sprechen Sie Deutsches?" Louis understood perfectly clearly that he was being asked in German if he spoke the German language, since he obviously had a German name. Louis did not respond and just kept his poker face looking straight into the officer's eyes. "What are you doing over here fighting your own people?" the SS officer then asked in perfect English. Louis did not answer—nothing he could say, as they were under strict orders to say only their name, rank, and serial number. Plus, there was nothing Louis could say because he really knew nothing!

Then the officer tapped him on the shoulder again as he inspected his 82nd Airborne insignia patch. "Devil in baggy pants?" he said, and then he mumbled something about respecting the 82nd since it had previously invaded Sicily too. "First historic jump into combat. Your outfit performed with great distinction and became known as the "fighting devils." Lots of respect was shown them by the Germans. This officer was no exception, and then he said, "Too bad you also lost many men to 'friendly fire' when the U.S. Navy shot down some of your planes loaded with paratroopers from the 82nd on their way to the drop in Sicily." Louis did not know if that was true or not. Then the SS officer moved on to the next interrogation. Sgt. Leidenheimer, who was standing near Louis, asked him what that was all about. Louis said he had no idea. The sergeant said that officer was most likely German SS Intelligence. Plus, since Louis was obviously of German ancestry, he chose him to just "mess with him" for a few moments.

The sergeant commended Louis for not revealing that he spoke and understood German, and keeping his cool during the interrogation. Then he asked Louis about his jump and what happened afterwards, both speaking very softly. Louis told the sergeant about the difficulty making the jump from the plane after the green light. The sergeant had been the first to jump and told Louis that after the first oscillation around as his parachute opened, he could see their plane was being tailed by a German ME-109 Messerschmitt fighter pumping 13 mm rounds into their loaded C-47. "No wonder we got shot to hell," he said. He went on to quietly tell Louis and several others standing nearby that their plane was the last one in their formation to come over the coast, so all the German flak batteries were up and firing everything they had. The sergeant went on to say it appeared that their unit, the 507th, seemed to have the worst drop of the entire regiment, most widely dispersed and at this point most casualties and captured.

As other captured paratroopers arrived, the group of prisoners of war (POWs) got even larger. Louis and the sergeant were now standing at the rear of the crowd of American POWs. Louis and the sergeant noted that the officer doing the interrogation could no longer see them, nor could any of the other guards. Louis looked around for a moment. When he looked back to his sergeant, he saw him just slip under the barn wall and into the darkness of the barn. Louis quietly watched through a crack in the siding, and in the darkness of the barn he could see his sergeant hide under a pile of farm implements near one corner of the barn.

Then, within another moment, a second POW also slipped under the barn wall. Louis, still quietly watching through the crack, saw this man climb into a wagon inside the barn to hide. However, now the German officer took note of a number of POWs looking and acting restless near the wall of the barn. The German SS officer ordered one of the guards to go into the barn and search it carefully. Inside the barn, the German guard discovered the unfortunate paratrooper hiding in the wagon and ordered him outside into the open. Next, the SS officer ordered two guards to beat this man with their rifle butts until he was no longer moving, or moaning.

Louis could not see the paratrooper lying on the ground as he was being beaten, due to the crowd of other POWs between them. But Louis could see the rifles rise and fall with each bone-crushing blow. He could hear the pounding impact of each thrust and felt he could even hear the crack of bones being broken or shattered with each heavy and vicious blow. The worst part was when the fellow POW stopped moaning with the agony and pain of the blows… when he became silent—either unconscious, or dead. Louis felt an impulse within him to sob…tears welled up in his eyes as the violent terror of the beating continued. Louis felt a sudden nausea in his stomach, sickened by the horror of the merciless beating and the depraved violence he was seeing. He was becoming overwhelmed by the terror and constant horror of all the death and suffering he had already witnessed in only a few days since entering combat. But this profound angst and sadness was also being slowly displaced by a growing numbness, a hardening to reconcile the constant hunger, pain, suffering, and death that stalked Louis, as it did all soldiers in combat—the unknowable question of who would be next? When would it be your turn to suffer or die?

Louis continued to wonder if a sudden death in combat would be a better fate than his present one—to be held captive by the enemy and live with the constant reality of death, and worst…the helplessness, the complete lack of power and control over your own destiny.

He could not tell if the beaten paratrooper was dead or alive, nor could any other POWs. The SS officer ordered the lifeless body of the man to be dragged away, and Louis never did learn what happened to him. The SS officer then made a loud and emphatic speech that anyone else caught attempting to escape would be killed on the spot—without hesitation. This depressing event made a profound impression on Louis and the others.

Louis made a point to pay no more attention to anything going on inside the barn to be certain not to draw the SS officer's attention back to his missing sergeant. Louis did not know if his sergeant made good his escape or not—he never saw him again after that afternoon.

Then a somewhat happy irony occurred to Louis: As everyone's attention was so focused on the poor paratrooper being beaten mercilessly, Louis realized that his sergeant, who was the first to slip under the barn wall, had surely used this diversion to make his getaway! By now he must have been a couple of miles away, and he, at least, would live to fight another day! That seems to be just how this madness of war works, Louis thought to himself. One man dies and another man lives.

But the violence of the beating was very sobering to Louis, and he began to think to himself of the great irony at work here. Several hundred years ago, his German ancestors left the German Rhineland by the hundreds and accepted an invitation from Catherine the Great, Empress of Russia, to relocate to the Volga River valley in Russia. One of the promises given to induce the Germans to move by the hundreds to Russia was the promise of exemption from military service for the Russian Empire. After seeing their sons go off to fight in the European wars for hundreds of years, with only a few ever returning, the German Rhinelanders jumped at the chance to live in peace.

Now, here I am, a direct ancestor of these peace-loving Germans, from Russia to America, and now back to Europe to fight the Germans! A crazy damn war, right? Louis thought to himself in silence.

There was fighting all around the area. All the 82nd and 101st Airborne outfits were really messed up. They were so spread out and disorganized. Yet, clearly, in spite of the confusion, they were giving the Germans a hellish fight, based on what Louis was hearing from other captives. Even from their present position as POWs, they could see toward the beaches of Normandy, and the entire sky glowed orange with light from the fires and the fighting.

As darkness took over the day, the POWs were told by their German guards they would sleep there tonight, on the ground, then move out in the morning. This was the first actual night's sleep since the jump on D-Day without worrying about being attacked or shot in your sleep. There in the cold darkness and relative stillness, with only the distant rumble of the ongoing war nearby, Louis' thoughts returned again to his early childhood and that other terrible night.

Chapter 6

Front page news

Louis watched, holding hands with his sister Jerry, as the men placed their mother's lifeless body into a wooden coffin and took it outside into the frigid wind to load into the funeral wagon. The memory of this event was seared into Louis' young mind and heart. A great sadness that would never leave him and haunt his every thought for the rest of his days. Icy tears streaked his face along with Jerry's as they stood on the porch, holding hands, with the frigid wind blowing across the frozen white, snow-covered fields. The glare of sunlight on the snow-covered land made them close their eyes, squeezing out more tears.

Their mother's body was taken into Hays to the funeral home to be prepared for her funeral. Then she would be brought to Grandma Pfeifer's home for the wake. The next day she would be taken to St. Joseph's Church for a Rosary and finally, the funeral Mass. All of this was so new to Louis and Jerry. It was all so very sad. Everyone was sad, and spoke in quiet, hushed whispers. But they also showed so much love and sympathy to little Louis and his sister Jerry, who was always at his side now. Neither was used to this much attention from adults.

Their dad was taken to Dr. Betthauser for attention to his frost-bitten fingers and toes; his lungs were very bad from breathing the frigid air, and he was snow-blind. He was in bad shape, the two kids kept hearing people say. But, a damn shame he could not make it home without saving Theresa too. This was also said so many times. The two young children did not understand. They were still grasping the fact that their mother was gone, never to return…in heaven with the angels, as people kept saying. Small comfort, Louis thought. I miss her so much already.

Grandma Pfeifer's first name was Cecelia, but that was a tongue twister for the little children in the family, so the grandkids always just called her Grandma "CC." She took the two youngest children, Louis and Jerry, home with her to Hays. Martina, Gene, Fred, and Marcel stayed at the farm along with their Aunt Maria to look after the stock.

Grandma CC had just finished giving Jerry and Louis a nice hot breakfast of oatmeal and cream when a knock was heard at the front door. Grandma CC opened the door to greet Mr. Kuhn, a reporter for the Hays newspaper. He explained that he wanted to check on the Pfeifer kids and get her thoughts on the events of the last night. Grandma CC knew Mr. Kuhn, a respected and well thought of man in the town. She invited him to take a chair at the kitchen table, offered him a bowl of hot oatmeal and a cup of coffee. Mr. Kuhn declined the oatmeal and accepted the hot coffee. Mr. Kuhn began to relate the story as he'd heard it earlier at the sheriff's office after Alex Pfeifer had given his statement to the sheriff and Dr. Betthauser.

"Mrs. Pfeifer, I understand that your son and his wife went to church yesterday evening for Mass on Ash Wednesday and left their six children home. The blizzard storm came in force just as they got out of church. While they only live five miles north of town, the conditions deteriorated so quickly that travel became extremely difficult. However, I understand they made it on the north road to within about one mile of the home. Yet, given the total darkness and the intense and blinding snow, they most likely had no real idea where they were or just how close they were to the home. They wandered for about three hours until Alex finally did make it to his home at 3 o'clock this morning. He immediately phoned his nearest neighbors to the east, who went out in the storm in search of Mrs. Pfeifer. Alex also said to them that he was going back out too, in search of his wife. The neighbor, Jake Walter, caught up with Alex soon after and found him snow-blind and in a helpless state. He said Alex would not have lasted much longer in this storm.

"By 6 o'clock this morning, Mrs. Pfeifer was found frozen to the ground under a barbwire fence in the wheat field only about one-half mile from the home. She was found in the deep snowdrifts because she had one hand reaching up and gripping the top stand of wire. That was all that was visible—that one gloved hand. Is this consistent with your understanding, Mrs. Pfeifer," Kuhn asked, looking up from his pad of notes taken earlier. "I understand the six children range in age from 2 to 12, is that right, Mrs. Pfeifer?" Mr. Kuhn asked.

"Yes, and the two youngest will stay with me, and other family will help the older children at the farm, as will I also when time permits."

"Some folks already seem very shocked and upset that Mr. Pfeifer was only able to save himself and not his wife too," Kuhn commented as he took another sip of coffee.

"I am certain my son did all he could, but after so many hours in frigid air, driving wind, and blinding snow, well others have succumbed to such conditions too, as you know," Mrs. Pfeifer responded.

"I do know that, and hypothermia can set in pretty fast under those extremely harsh conditions too. I have asked Dr. Betthauser about that just this morning. He said the first symptom is usually confusion and sleepiness, which can contribute to disorientation, not knowing where you are, or where you are going. Then shallow breathing and slow speech, a weaker pulse, or irregular heartbeat, which sets the stage for extreme fatigue. Plus compulsive shivering that will not stop as the body core temperature drops. Finally, stiffness and numbness in the limbs takes over, making it very difficult to continue. I understand the greatest risk is sudden heart failure as the cold blood reaches the heart. Or, when a person gets inside and the sudden change in temperature gets the heart to fail. Few people could understand what the hard wind and frigid cold can do to a person unless they have been there themselves," Kuhn said.

Grandma CC had been so absorbed in Mr. Kuhn's comments, she lost her awareness for a moment that the two grandchildren, Louis and Jerry, were still sitting at the table listening. Their eyes were so wide open and wet—they had stopped eating and just sat there listening. "What else can I do for you this morning, Mr. Kuhn?" she said as her eyes glanced from him to the two children, signaling to him a need to be mindful of the children and how this ordeal was affecting them.

"Well, the rain and snow of yesterday will sure stop those hellish dust storms we have had continuously for the past ten days!" Mr. Kuhn commented with an optimistic tone, to try to cheer up the air in the kitchen.

"That is one blessing," Grandma CC agreed as she re-filled his coffee cup.

"Based on the early reports so far today, the heaviest rain and snow fell north of Hays, where the Alex Pfeifer farm is located. Plus, so much more around Hays than there was to the south, east, or west of us. It will be a wonderful benefit to the area farmers and the spring wheat crop, no doubt about that too," Kuhn continued, still keeping it positive for the sake of the kids. Grandma CC's eyes flashed another note of aggravation to Mr. Kuhn for relating the helpful moisture to the farmers in front of two children who had just lost their mother to this terrible blizzard. But, oblivious to this, Mr. Kuhn just kept talking as he was walked to the door to leave.

"Things are sure tied up here in town too. Phone lines are out all over the area, with only two circuits out of 17 still working. Plus the midnight eastbound train did not arrive until about eight o'clock this morning. It has even stopped the mail today. No postal carriers will be able to make their routes today. Cars and trucks are useless, only a horse or wagon can move today. But, the good news is the shovelers are out in force since before daylight clearing the sidewalks around town.

"Got another story I am just now working on too. It seems that old John Schlyer passed away last night too. He came to Hays in 1868 to hunt buffalo and, as you know, held many positions in public service over the years here in Hays," Mr. Kuhn said, as he put on his hat and heavy overcoat. Then he opened the door to leave, thanking Mrs. Pfeifer for her hospitality. He gave Louis and Jerry a pat on the head and walked through the open door and out into the bright, frigid morning.

Grandma CC pushed the door closed with a finality that made it clear to Louis and Jerry that she was glad to see him go. So were they. "Well, who wants a bath?" Grandma asked the two brown-eyed kids standing in front of her. They looked at each other, then both turned and ran away—inviting Grandma CC to catch them if she could....

Chapter 7

Why be a paratrooper?

"Louis, why the hell did you sign up with the 82nd Airborne? Look where it has gotten you," James asked Louis the next morning as they sat on the ground waiting for the German guards to make the next move.

"I did it for the boots," Louis answered. He went on to explain that he spent most of his childhood going barefoot and always appreciated a really good pair of shoes.

In fact, he thought back for a moment to one of the first letters he wrote to his sister Jerry just after she had left the St. Joseph's orphanage in Abilene, Kansas, to live with their Aunt Marie in Kansas City. He told Jerry in that letter that if she happened to come into any extra money that she could spare, would she send it to him so he could buy a new pair of shoes? Louis had no shoes at that point in time because he had worn out and outgrown his last pair. That was the summer of 1935, Louis thought to himself. Jerry was only 12 years old, and I was just 11.... So, where did I think she was going to come up with any money anyway? Louis smiled as he remembered those other hard times. Then he also remembered his reasoning was that he and Jerry each always helped the other, whenever they could, however they could. In those days they only had each other.

Louis continued, quietly to James, "Besides, the paratrooper boots were special. They laced up all the way to the top. No hooks. And a paratrooper wears his pants tucked inside his boots, which really showed off those great boots. Kept them shiny black too. Made a few regular GIs a little jealous and more than a few fistfights started over those boots. But, the girls really like them too, you know." James nodded in agreement as they both looked down at the muddy, scuffed up boots they now wore, then looked at each other and smiled the same ironic smile they seemed to repeat so often in the past few days.

"Yeah, but they really got me in trouble when we left the states," Louis recalled quietly to James. When we were marched onto a dock alongside the Queen Mary. She was such a beautiful ship. I really hoped that would be our boat to sail for England. But instead we lined up in front of the HMS Strathnaver, an old British transport ship. Well, our boots have those very hard heels that popped when you slapped them together. So, as we marched to a halt, I clicked my heels together with a loud pop! Just like the Germans are trained to do, you know?

"Got me in a ton of trouble. The captain called me into his cabin. He asked me why I was pulling crap like that. Then he asked me what we should do about this? So, I mouthed off and said, 'Push-ups, of course, Sir!' But my first lieutenant, who was dying to be made captain and was also in the cabin, said, 'You will pull guard duty on two-up shifts for six hours until you are relieved, for the entire trip to England.' Not that bad a punishment, I thought. Spent lots of time on deck marching around. Got to see the Statue of Liberty as we left the harbor. Beautiful and inspiring. But, I also wondered if I would ever see it again."

"Sure, Louis, I remember that well—you were always getting in trouble with that jocular sense of humor of yours!" James whispered.

Speaking of that first lieutenant, Louis remembered that he seemed to have it in for him anyway. Most likely due to the same encounter when Louis fell flat on his face while he and James had been drinking a pint of whiskey during the movie in Alliance, Nebraska, where they did their basic training for paratrooper qualifications. Just as they left the theatre, the lieutenant had also walked out and stopped to speak to them for a moment. Just then, a pigeon flew over and dropped a splash of pigeon crap right on the lieutenant's shoulder patch. Louis thought the splotch of pigeon poop looked like a major's insignia so he said, "Looks like you just got promoted to lieutenant—MAJOR!" Everyone got a good laugh from that one, except the lieutenant...who took it as disrespect and never forgot, nor forgave, Louis' comment.

Louis continued to remember the route that got him to where he now found himself:

The old ship they sailed across the Atlantic on had already survived several torpedo attacks. As Louis marched all over the ship on guard duty, he often went down into the hold. There were many Indian people doing most of the work, and they wore small red hats. But mainly Louis remembered the food they ate. It was horrible!

During the entire crossing, Louis would no more lie down in a bunk when someone would wake him and say, "Pfeifer, you got to go back on guard duty!"

Beginning 23 November 1943, it took a month for the regiment to get settled into Portrush, Northern Ireland, via Camp Shanks and Fort Hamilton, NY, the British Ship HMS Strathnaver to Liverpool, the Liberty ship Susan B. Anthony to Belfast. Only small unit training could be done there to keep the edge on the trooper skills.

"I figured you signed up for the great pay, Louis, right?" James said, continuing the conversation with a hint of sarcasm. "It was really about that buck a day, or 80 cents per hour, plus $50 for jumping—and only five jumps to qualify. Piece of cake, right?"

"No, I only wanted the boots," Pfeifer replied with a slight smile on his face. Then, Louis remembered how he'd lied about his age to enlist in the army when he was only 17 years old. His dad even signed for him to back up the lie! Now Louis wondered what had made him so anxious to get into this war. Oh, everyone else was doing it too, and patriotism was rampant across the country. No regrets, Louis thought to himself; whatever happens, he and so many others are doing their duty to protect their country and loved ones back home.

"Aufmerksamkeit! Stehen Sie auf und aufstellen! Antworten Sie auf Rolle, wenn Ihr Name genannt wird!"

a German officer yelled. Then the order was repeated in English, "Attention, stand up and line up, then answer roll when your name is called!"

Louis heard him the first time and fully understood before the English translation, and he began to stand up, and then realized he was the only one standing and quickly set back down! Whew! Louis thought to himself, better be careful—it is just that easy to blow his cover that he spoke German. Not a good idea for either side at this point.

Before long the entire company of about 500 American and British POWs was marching down the road out of Cherbourg under German guard. First they marched south, then east along the coast. The column of POWs marched all day until they arrived at Allen pond. Then the Germans finally fed them. A pile of slop was dropped onto a pie plate and handed to each of the POWs. Louis took one taste and spit it out, then threw the plate away. Later on he wished he had eaten it, but he had no idea then how hungry he would become later. At night they told the POWs to take off their belts and shoelaces and turn them in to the guards. Guess they figured it would be hard for the POWs to run away holding their pants up and with their boots flopping off.

The next morning the POW column was at it again, marching further east, inland toward Paris and the trains, as they were told by one guard who was friendly enough to share that information. There was constant fighting of aircraft in the sky above them. As they marched along the road, it went through an apple orchard with trees growing along both sides. Louis, like all the captive soldiers, was starving. The sight of the red apples on the trees looked simply irresistible. Plus many apples had already fallen to the ground and were softened to rotten in the June sunshine. The scent of those apples was so delicious and tempting, Louis thought it might be worth getting shot just to fall on the ground and swallow as many as he could in his last moments here on earth....

Suddenly, the head of a man just a few yards ahead of Louis just blew off! Other men fell, and bodies began to explode as an American P-51 Mustang strafed the POW column. The screams of agony by the men being hit could be heard along with the oppressive roar of the P-51 Rolls Royce Merlin engines. Louis instinctively dove for cover on the ground and hugged the nearest apple tree. A second and then a third P-51 came over and strafed them again. Louis could see them just peeling off, then coming in low for the strafing run. He could see the bursts of fire and smoke coming off their wings, and you knew they were firing their guns at the POWs by mistake. Our own planes killed about 135 POWs that day and yet, only two German guards were killed by the strafing planes.

When they stopped, at last, the air was fogged with a mist of dust, blood, and apple tree leaves. Men were moaning in agony. Louis realized he was feeling a hot burning sensation on his left foot. He sat up and looked at his foot. There was a black scorch mark along the side of his boot where a 50-caliber shell had just grazed his boot. Lord, I came so close to cashing in, just a few more inches to the right and it would be all over for me, Louis thought to himself. He sat there for a moment and watched one of the guys staggering around in shock—his arm was just hanging from his shoulder by a shred of skin.

Strafe, Louis thought to himself. Understanding German, Louis realized the root German word meant to "punish." Well, it certainly applied in this instance. The strafing happened so fast and was so totally devastating, Louis was still feeling the most intense terror he had ever felt in his life. He found himself searching the sky with upturned eyes, dreading another attack, straining his ears to hear any distant roar of more incoming planes. It took several moments for the shock to pass. Then the German guards began to organize themselves and the POWs.

The Germans ordered the POWs to gather the wounded into a nearby barn. It was getting late and that would be their cover for the night. Several POWs, starving like the rest of them, picked up apples on the ground or off the trees. A German guard saw this and hit one prisoner with his rifle butt. "Lassen Sie es fallen! Kein Diebstahl!" the guard said. Then another officer yelled a translation, "Drop it, no stealing! Anyone caught stealing food will be shot!" he added.

James was standing behind Louis and whispered, "Lousy Germans, you would think this was their own farm."

"Maybe they think all of France belongs to them," Louis whispered back. But, silently to himself, Louis felt some respect for the Germans to not allow anyone to steal the farmer's fruit, even under war conditions. Louis noted to himself that none of the German guards helped themselves to any of the apples either. Not even those rotting on the ground.

Later that night, in the dark, men were lying all over the ground. Only officers and some wounded were allowed shelter in the barn. One private who was badly wounded was lying near Louis. He asked Louis to get his wallet out of his pocket and pull out the picture he carried of his wife and son. Louis did this and handed him the picture. Louis did not know this man, but listened as he explained that the child in the picture was his newborn son. The child was born after he had shipped out. He had never seen his son and worried that now he never would. The private died just a short time later, still holding the picture of his wife and new son. Louis was lying right beside him and heard him take his last breath.

Louis felt a deepening despair. Death haunted him and seemed to surround him. The terror of living with the constant possibility of death, from so many sources, each as unpredictable as the next...filled Louis with a quiet terror. It was hard to sleep. Very hard to settle his mind down and relax enough to sleep.

He lay there under the stars and searched his memory for a happier time to think about until sleep relieved him of this day's horrors. He began to remember the days after his mother died when he and his older sister Jerry were sent to live in town with their beloved Grandma Pfeifer. Yet, it was hard to think of those good days without remembering the beginning, the first days without his mother, Theresa, in his life....

Chapter 8

The Volga-Germans

Grandma CC Pfeifer was a large woman with a towering presence over Louis and his sister Jerry. But she was a true gentle giant in their eyes. Louis never felt more loved by anyone in his life from her gentle smile to soft touch and caring manner, except when he experienced the same from his older sister Jerry. In fact, in so many ways they were very much alike. Grandma Pfeifer never got upset, was always very patient, and never failed to do whatever was in their best interests. She always called Louis "Sonny." But Louis always thought she meant "Sunny"—to encourage him to embrace the same "sunny" disposition as his sister Jerry, and also as herself.

Grandma CC had lost her husband, Johannes Adam Pfeifer, Louis and Jerry's grandfather, to lung problems in October 1917. He arrived in New York in 1878 from Bremen, Germany, on the SS Leipzig. Then made his way to the plains of western Kansas along with hundreds of other Volga-Germans. Johannes Adam Pfeifer was born May 10, 1859 in Herzog, Samara, Russia. He married his first wife, Paulina Mueller, on September 9, 1879. She was 18 years old and he was 20 years old. That same day, Johannes sister, Anna Margareta Pfeifer, married Alexander Rupp. Sadly, Johannes' wife, Paulina, died in childbirth along with her child on February 25, 1883.

Cecelia Rupp arrived in New York on August 3, 1876 aboard the SS Suevia from Hamburg and Havre. She traveled to the New World in hope of a new life, along with the rest of her family, including her brother, Alexander Rupp. She was only 11 years old when she arrived in the United States from her homeland in Ober-Munjou, Samara, Russia.

On April 3, 1883, Johannes Adam Pfeifer married Cecelia Rupp. He was then 24 and she was 18 years old. This was now the second marriage between the two families. They had 11 children, but one only lived three years. They raised ten of their children to adulthood, including Louis' father, Alex.

Grandpa Johannes Adam Pfeifer was a very successful farmer. He had taken the train to California to try to find a cure for his lung problems. He had done so well as a farmer during World War I that he became known as "Rich Pfeifer" by his German friends. However other townsfolk, well maybe they were a little jealous of the success of the Pfeifer family, as his son Alex would later come to terms with in his life. But Grandpa Johannes Adam was so rich that when each of his sons left home and got married, he gave them an 80-acre farm free and clear.

Eventually Louis' dad, Alex, worked his holdings up to 400 acres, but it was not the best land. He lost it all during the Depression and due to other troubles he had with the local law enforcement in town.

One of the first things Louis learned from his Grandma CC Pfeifer was to know and understand who they were as

a family, and how and why they came to America. She only spoke German, so Louis and Jerry heard all this in their own native German tongue too. "I was born Cecelia Rupp on November 11, 1865 in Ober-Munjou (Ksriwowskoje) at Samara, Russia…." Grandma Pfeifer-Rupp would always start her stories about the family history the same way.

"It was in the later years in school when English became their spoken daily language. At this time in our life, we were German Americans and spoke German at home. But, the anti-German sentiment in the United States after World War I, or the "Great War" as they called it before World War II began, made learning to speak English an essential fact of life." Still, Grandma CC was proud of her German heritage and wanted to be certain Louis and Jerry knew it well. Especially that they were German; even though their families spent about 200 years living in Russia, they never stopped being German, and always kept to their faith, customs, and traditions as German people.

After her husband, Johannes, passed away in 1917, Grandma CC Pfeifer moved into town. She bought a complete platted city block of land, built a charming home with plans she had ordered from Russia, on the corner of 15th Street and Walnut, and sold off lots to support herself as the years went by.

She often told Jerry and Louis the history of their German people, who came to be called the "Volga-Germans." *Louis let the story roll over in his mind again as he lay there under the stars in France, being held captive as a prisoner of war by German soldiers who might actually be descendants from common ancestors of his. Hell! He might even be related to these men! How ironic all this war is...!*

The Volga River runs through the Samara and Saratov regions in southeastern Russia. In the years 1763 to 1767, the reigning empress of Russia, Catherine II, or Catherine the Great as history came to refer to her, invited German families to come to this area to settle. They were offered generous grants of land to occupy, self-governing rights, religious freedom, and most important at that time, exemption from military service. The wars of Europe had raged for centuries and families regularly saw their young sons called off to the armies at war only to never return. So, one of the great inducements offered by Empress Catherine II was exemption from military service for an indefinite period of time. The German settlers were also given a limited 30-year exemption from taxes and the guarantee of religious freedom.

Russia's empress was anxious to populate the newly acquired territory of the Volga River valley and the Black Sea region. The industrious Germans seemed ideal and a fine alternative to the lawless barbarian hordes presently occupying this area. Plus, Empress Catherine was also of German ancestry, and well aware of the close family bonds and traditions of hard work these German folk were known to possess.

Over time nearly 8,000 families, about 25,000 people, moved into the Volga valley from Germany. They settled over 100 colonies. Yet, while living in Russia, they retained their German language, customs, and traditions. They prospered

under their own communal governments and enjoyed the freedom from military service. But it was too good to last.

The east side of the Volga was a wild and virgin steppe country, while the west side was more rugged and hilly. The only native occupants were the equally wild and rugged nomadic tribes of the Kirgiz hordes. These semi-barbarian tribes resented and preyed upon the new German settlers. Frequent raids on the settlements resulted in burning, murder, theft, and being carried off into captivity.

Eventually the Russian military intervened and delivered a crushing defeat upon the Kirgiz tribes. That led to a period where the colonies could grow and prosper in relative peace for many years to follow. In fact, the German colonies soon outgrew their native Russian counterparts in prosperous opulence. Envy and resentment towards the successful Germans soon arose among the native Russians in the area. Not the least of which, the exemption from military service was another cause for resentment.

In January 1874, Russia, under the rule of Tsar Alexander II, a new law was passed making all colonists of military age subject to military service, including and especially the German colonists. The Crimean Wars had taken a terrible toll on the Russian people in loss of life and this was no small factor in fueling even more resentment toward the military-exempt colonists from Germany.

Then in 1880, another law was passed making the Russian language mandatory in all the German colonies, especially all schools. Clearly the tide was changing for the Volga-Germans who could see only more pressure to adopt the Russian culture and customs in place of their own cherished culture and traditions.

An earlier exemption from military service, limited to only ten years, had been passed in 1871, providing, however, that during that period the colonists could immigrate to any other country without loss of their property in Russia.

With these developments, growing uncertainty about the future of the German colonies in Russia led to a meeting in Hertzog to examine the situation and consider what alternative course of action might be open to the colonies. The meeting selected five delegates to visit the United States and explore the Nebraska territory as a possible new home. By November 1875 the first group of Volga-German settlers arrived, but in Topeka, Kansas, and not Nebraska. By the spring of 1876 these families set out for Ellis County, Kansas, and began to establish settlements in the area surrounding Fort Hays.

At this time, Fort Hays was a frontier settlement, anchored and protected by the venerable Seventh Calvary stationed at Fort Hays. Yet, still a true frontier town, with historic characters like Wyatt Earp, Buffalo Bill, and Wild Bill Hickok playing a role in the town's history. Grandpa and Grandma Pfeifer came of age and raised their large family of six boys and four girls, after the loss of one child at three years of age, right in the midst of all this history.

By the time Louis was ready to start school, he knew this history backwards and forwards. He was proud of his German heritage, and equally proud to be an American-

German now too. But, within the town and essentially across the country, Germans were not that well liked and a strong current of resentment over the first Great War still existed.

Looking back over his short life, the time with Grandma CC was just the best. But it was too good to last.

Chapter 9

Haunted by hunger under the stars

L ouis lay there under the stars—among the dead, wounded, and dying, along with others like him who still lived, if only for one day at a time. Louis found himself remembering the remarkable story about the death of old John Schlyer.

It had always seemed amazing to Louis that on the same night his mother and father struggled to make it home in that terrible snowstorm, Frank Schlyer, the son of old man John Schlyer, had gotten word of his father's death. He set out from Stockton to Hays in his car, a distance of just under 40 miles. The snowdrifts were so deep he soon abandoned his car near the Ellis county line, still about 20 miles from Hays. Then he continued on foot. He arrived at a farm near Hays about 2:00 A.M., where he spent the night. The next day, the roads still impassable, he continued through the deep snowdrifts on foot until he arrived at Hays around noon. He had covered about 18 miles on foot, in one of the worst snowstorms in recent memory, just to attend his father's funeral. He did this the same night Louis' father and mother could not cover less than one mile from their car in the ditch to the warmth and safety of their farmhouse.

Louis remembered how the morning of his mother's death, he could stand on the front porch of the house and see the 1922 Ford Model T that his father drove lying in the ditch on the road just about one mile east of their house. But the only way to travel for days after that storm was by horse-drawn wagon. The snowdrifts were so deep, it was just impossible to travel by car.

As Louis lay there under the stars somewhere in France, he could still hear the muffled sound of gunfire off in the distance. They had marched far enough from the front that the battle action was becoming more remote. But the squadrons of bombers were still flying overhead, and occasional squadrons of fighter escorts still roaring past overhead too. But eventually, late into the evening, things would quiet down enough that sleep seemed possible.

Again, Louis began to think of the irony of his situation. He had as much reason to fear death or injury from the sky when the Allied bombers flew overhead, and their escort fighters. From their viewpoint, up in the sky flying 200 or more miles per hour, they took the uniformed cluster of POWs for a ragtag collection or column of retreating Germans, so constant strafing runs were likely at any time. But the more immediate death threat came from the German guards around the POWs.

They were a mixed group. Some seemed reasonable, fair, not too threatening, but still serious and duty bound to follow orders. And their orders were to shoot to kill any prisoners who tried to escape or failed to follow orders. Other Germans, however, seemed very bitter toward the Americans, and they seemed to relish their role as POW guards. These bitter Germans would kill on a whim. At this point, Louis was never really certain which type he was dealing with on any occasion. So, he began to live with the constant awareness that each breath, each moment, each blink of his eye could be his last here on earth.

As these thoughts floated through Louis' mind, he again smelled the sweet scent of the apple orchard nearby. He remembered the sweet ripe apples hanging on the trees and littered about the ground. He fantasized for just a moment that maybe he could crawl on his belly without being seen back up the road to that orchard and eat his fill. Then fill his pockets with apples to share with James and his other buddies nearby. James! Louis just realized he had not seen his buddy James all day. His preoccupation was with hunger, mindless marching, and constant vigilance toward the sky for the next airplane, friend or foe, that might dive on and strafe or bomb their column. A moment of panic for James rose in Louis' heart. Did James get killed in one of the strafing runs? Had he been shot by a German guard? Somehow they had been separated. Louis resolved to try to locate James in the morning....

Then his thoughts returned to his most immediate feelings. Hunger consumed his body and he ached for something to eat—anything would do. Then a German guard walked by slowly doing his night patrol of the POWs. Louis saw the glint of light flash off his bayonet fixed to his Mausher rifle. For an instant Louis imagined himself crawling silently up the ditch along the side of the road to retrieve as many apples as he could, and what it would feel like to suddenly have that bayonet plunged into his back, and through him into the ground, pinning him to the ground like a butterfly pinned to a piece of cardboard.

Louis closed his eyes and retreated back into his memories of the wonderful times at Grandma CC Pfeifer's home and the food she cooked; ah—the wonderful German cooking he'd enjoyed there.

Breakfast at Grandma's nearly always included fresh onion bread. Louis remembers waking up early in the morning to the scent of buttered onions cooking on the stove in a cast-iron skillet. Then, when the freshly kneaded dough was ready, the hot buttered onions were layered across the middle of the bread dough. The dough was then rolled up by Grandma CC into a jelly-roll manner so the steaming buttered onions became a spiral of flavor inside the fresh hot bread. Everyone got up promptly on those days and would be waiting at the table when the hot buttered onion bread came out of the oven. There were never any leftovers of that fresh, hot onion bread.

Louis continued to use his memory of food to remedy his intense hunger for real food, and moved onto one of his favorite soups made by Grandma Pfeifer. The sour cream soup, with hefty chunks of potatoes, green beans, and onions, laced with a dash of allspice or nutmeg—oh, that was so simple and yet so wonderful. But the typical soup that was most commonly set on the table was Weisse Bohensuppe—just plain old white bean soup. It always included ham hocks, onions, carrot bits, celery, and a hint of garlic or clove, but the ham hocks, they were Louis' favorite. They would be so tender after boiling with the beans that the meat would just fall away from the bones.

Louis asked himself to stop—this borders on personal torture, he quietly thought to himself; why go on? Then his mind answered by saying to himself, because the best is yet to come…. Remember dessert? Louis asked himself, silently remembering. Those wonderful Lebkuchen—German honey cakes, just loaded with honey, brown sugar, hint of lemon, nutmeg, clove, and cinnamon—plus shredded almonds too, if they were available. Oh my God, Louis thought; he could smell them just then, fresh from the oven. He was a little boy again, gathered to the table and waiting with his cup of milk to eat his fill.

Finally, in the very quiet darkness, Louis let his mind travel back to America. He imagined himself back in Kansas City at Jerry's house. He wondered what she was doing at that moment. He imagined it must be dinnertime and what was she putting on the table? Jerry learned to cook from the early days at Grandma Pfeifer's home, and she could manage all the great German recipes. Perhaps tonight it was Schnitzel, or pork loin cutlets with sauerkraut, red cabbage, and potato dumplings. Yet, as much as Louis hungered for food, the thought of his dear sister, who had been his constant companion during his childhood, took over his feelings and longings. He craved the warmth and security of her company, and the unconditional love and mutual support between them. They always took care of each other, and whatever one had, they would share with the other.

Louis said a silent prayer and quietly fell asleep thinking of his beloved sister, Jerry.

Chapter 10

Train ride to nowhere

When Louis awoke the next morning, his mind was still back in time to Kansas City and the times at Jerry's house, then further back to the wonderful years at Grandma CC Pfeifer's home. But as Louis stood up and stretched along with his fellow POWs, he realized the stench they, as a group, were beginning to acquire. His uniform was caked with mud and dirt. It was becoming stiff and coarse, and made his skin chafe in the places where skin and fabric rubbed together.

Then Louis remembered with a smile, things were not always that great at Grandma CC's home either. Aunt Betty, Grandma CC's youngest daughter, and her husband, Roscoe, also lived with her at that time. It was a tough time for many, but not like the Great Depression that would come in the next decade of the 1930s. The 1920s had seen wheat prices generally rise year after year, and most farmers prospered. This prosperity meant growth and opportunity for others who made their living in a more risky manner. Gambling was one such endeavor that seemed to feed off this newfound wealth of the 1920s.

Yet, gamblers, like so many living off the success of others, often needed a base to build upon, until they could afford to stand on their own feet. So many families shared their homes with other family members for these reasons. Some were born out of the hardship of the times, and others simply out of necessity. This was typical of Grandma CC and her huge heart—she took in anyone who needed help and shelter, including Louis and his sister Jerry. "That is what family is all about," she would say, and she would just swing the door wide open with a welcome hug and a smile, and then head for the kitchen to make a large meal for the new houseguests.

So, Grandma CC had also taken in her youngest daughter, Aunt Betty, and Roscoe, her husband. Roscoe was a man's man, a likable sort, who enjoyed talking, smoking, drinking, and most of all, gambling. Everyone seemed to like Uncle Roscoe. However, Aunt Betty, on the other hand, was quiet and spoke softly most of the time, but like most of the Pfeifer's, you did not want to make her mad!

Still, Louis' life up to that point had given him a fair share of heartache and frustration, and as a result he too had developed a pretty good temper and a short fuse—just like his dad, some would say. Later, Louis came to realize it just ran in the family.

But as Louis was scratching around inside his crusty uniform, he thought back to the time he'd got so mad at his beloved sister, Jerry, that he gathered up all her doll clothes and her only precious dolly and ran down into the basement and tossed them into the roaring flame of the coal-fired furnace. Louis tried, but he just could not remember what Jerry did to upset him so much that he would do such a terrible thing. Louis still felt guilty just to think about this heinous act on his part. He loved his sister Jerry so much, and she was never anything but good, kind, and loving to him, as well as everyone else in her life. Yet, he was mad, and true to his Pfeifer nature, he did do this awful act.

Uncle Roscoe, Aunt Betty's husband, was down in the basement playing poker with his fellow poker friends. This was what uncle Roscoe did for a living in those days. He kept a poker game going in the basement of Grandma Pfeifer's house. Well, his presence led to Louis' immediate punishment from his wife, Aunt Betty.

Grandma CC was not home, so Aunt Betty was in charge of the house. She heard Uncle Roscoe's urgent summons to get that kid the hell out of the basement! Aunt Betty rushed downstairs, saw the glowing embers and remnants of Jerry's doll and doll clothes in the furnace, and jerked Louis by the arm all the way up the stairs. "You will sit in this corner!" she said as she shoved a chair into the corner and slammed Louis down into the chair. "I will teach you to respect other people's property!"

Jerry was already crying—for the loss of her dolly and all her doll clothes too. But when she saw Aunt Betty jerk Louis around and shove him into the chair in the corner, her tears became pleading to Aunt Betty to please not be mad at poor little Louis. Well, at this point, Aunt Betty was not interested in anything but achieving a measure of peace in the house! Mainly to keep her husband happy so he could continue to host a poker game in the basement and make his living unmolested by the chaos of two quarreling little kids.

Jerry was then set in a chair in the other corner of the room, crying inconsolably, while also begging Aunt Betty to not punish either of them anymore. Such was the great love and compassion she had for Louis, her little brother, even after he had destroyed her most precious possessions.

But, ignoring both of them and their tears, Aunt Betty set to work at the sewing machine, and within a matter of about 20 minutes she said, "There, this will teach Louis a lesson or two." Louis turned his head from the corner and saw Aunt Betty holding up what looked like a pair of long underwear, made to about his size. Except unlike normal underwear that was made from soft cotton, this garment was made from burlap! Louis knew instantly that he was in for it! Within another minute or two, there Louis was sitting back in the corner, wearing that burlap underwear!

It is very hard to describe the feeling that burlap underwear had, Louis thought to himself as the POWs marched along the road. But the crusty uniform scraping against his chaffing skin came pretty close. Louis remembered sitting in that chair with the burlap touching his skin. Even just the motion of his breathing would rub slightly against the burlap and the burning itch would begin. The only relief Louis got was that Aunt Betty would take it off him just before time for Grandma Pfeifer to return home, because she would never tolerate such punishment in her presence. But Louis was still too young to tell Grandma and brave the wrath of his Aunt Betty. So, nothing was said. And for the next several years, if Louis misbehaved while Grandma was gone, Aunt Betty would pull the burlap suit from its hiding place and on it went. Louis learned to really be good during those times. Burlap underwear was a great motivator.

Suddenly, Louis and the other POWs were distracted again by the sound of aircraft overhead. After being strafed the other day, that sound held a particular edge of terror. You did not always hear them coming, they had learned. If they came from behind or in front, low and fast, the bullets often started exploding bodies before you could hear the engines roar overhead, and the planes would race past just over the treetops. But this time it was a flight of US P-51 fighter planes off to the right. One P-51 did peel off and turn back to come in low over the staggering marching column from front to rear. Many dropped to the ground for cover. Some just stood and waved in hopes of showing a sign of friendliness that we were not enemy Germans. A few of them even waved the little patch of colored cloth paratroopers were given to wave to fighter planes in the air to show they were allied troops. Whatever the reason, perhaps the uniforms not matching, or the lack of weapons, or the staggering haphazard formation of our column, the P-51 did not fire on them. He just flew over once and returned to his squadron formation and headed east toward Germany or whatever their mission was that day.

Louis realized as the squadron of P-51s flew off to continue their mission without strafing their column of POWs that he had broken out into a cold sweat of terror and fear as he'd first heard the roaring sound of the plane coming in low overhead. The instant flashback of the sudden carnage from the other day filled him with terror that did not quickly subside. Up to that point in his life, there was only one other noise that filled his heart with such terror. The mind-numbing, sense-crushing sound of a Kansas tornado….

Louis remembered the first time he and his sister Jerry experienced that tornado sound and the terror it raised in your heart. It was during the later years at Grandma CCs home. Louis, Jerry, and other kids in the neighborhood were playing outside around the house. The sky was growing dark, and the clouds began to look sinister and angry… rolling and boiling, with an energy that seemed to swell like an angry spirit in the sky. Louis and Jerry and the other kids noticed the wind was blowing harder—the wind was always blowing in Kansas. It was when the wind stopped blowing that you worried. The hard blowing wind was also becoming more chilled and swirling in circles…then the wind suddenly just stopped. The sky was totally black now, not dust storm black, but boiling grey black, with a weird greenish tone to the color—especially toward the southwest. The calming of the wind was what made the kids stop playing and take notice—the sudden change to stillness made their instincts of self-preservation take over. Then they heard the call of their Grandma CC from the front porch to come quickly into the house, they were all going to the basement! Jerry turned and ran toward the house. Louis did not. He just stood there staring at the boiling greenish black clouds. They were fascinating to Louis, who at this point did not understand and had no real fear of tornados, even though they were a fairly common phenomenon in the county.

Jerry stopped running and looked back when she realized Louis was still standing at the edge of the yard watching the sky full of boiling green-black clouds. Lightning flashed nearby with a crack that nearly knocked Louis and Jerry off their feet. Grandma CC, still standing on the porch, yelled to Jerry with a panic-filled voice, "Jerry, honey! Get Louis and come inside NOW!"

Jerry ran back and took Louis by the hand, pulling him with all her strength toward the porch. Louis, still fascinated by the rising spectacle in the sky, ran reluctantly, still watching over his shoulder. Another crack of lightning and the rolling roar of thunder filled the sky just as Jerry and Louis climbed the steps to the front porch. Marble-sized hail began to fall in that instant like someone had just pulled a switch in heaven and said, "Now let the ice balls fall!"

Louis thought the marble-sized hail was fascinating too and stopped on the porch to watch this spectacle too, but by now Grandma CC had his and Jerry's hands, and when this large woman pulled you by the hand, you followed without hesitation! Through the front screen door, across the parlor, with the wind blowing the sheer summer curtains like sails into the room through the open windows....

As everyone scrambled down the steps into the basement, the lights went out! The electricity had been knocked out by the storm, most likely due to the lightning, or wind, or hail. Uncle Roscoe was already in the basement along with Aunt Betty, and he had lit a kerosene lantern in anticipation of the lights going out. A common experience to those older and wiser in the area, like Uncle Roscoe.

As the family huddled close in the basement, Louis and the others began to hear the dull low rumble of thunder that did not stop. It continued to rumble. Worse, and more fearful than the thunder noise, was the fact that this noise did not end like thunder... no, it continued, and as it continued it would build in volume like a monster growling a low guttural roar, and only grew louder because it was coming closer with each second. Louis felt a crushing terror fill his heart and mind. He looked over to Jerry, held tightly in her Grandma CC's arms. Jerry had her eyes closed, but in the dim light of the kerosene lantern Louis could see tears running down Jerry's cheeks. Tears of terror, Louis thought. Seeing Jerry's tears made Louis start to cry too.

The roar in the sky continued for several minutes, getting louder and louder until it sounded like a hundred steam locomotives rushing along rails in the sky at full speed. It was the loudest sound Louis had ever heard at that point in his life. If a sound could kill you, just by crushing you, that was this tornado sound.

Then, just as Louis thought the entire house would be crushed on top of them and into the basement, the sound began to fade...quicker than it began, and within another moment, it was gone. All were silent in the basement. It took each a moment to recover their senses and return to the present. Roscoe spoke first: "I think that twister was close, but it sounded like it was maybe a half mile or so west of us, along the edge of town... sure hope no one was hurt."

Jerry spoke next in a quiet whisper, from her throat choked with terror. "Grandma, what was that, a tornado, or cyclone?"

"Yes, dear, they are both the same thing. And if you ever hear that sound again, you must go to shelter and take Louis with you too. Do not ever delay!" she said emphatically as she stroked Jerry's hair and looked at Louis with a rare scolding expression in her eyes. Grandma CC was still peeved with Louis for holding back in his fascination with the developing storm and not obeying her—especially after she had called for him to come in…but her heart being soft and her nature of forgiveness taking over, she said, "At least now we are all safe and sound," as she pulled Louis close and hugged him along with Jerry into her big soft bosom.

"You do not want to end up like the two Pfeifer children who were killed by a tornado many years ago!" Aunt Betty added, with her own scolding tone.

"Two children were killed?" Louis and Jerry both said, as each huddled closer to Grandma CC's embrace in the dimly lit basement.

"Yes, the two children were out playing in the farmyard when their parents heard and saw the tornado approach. They had little warning as it dropped right out of the sky near their farm. The parents called to the children to run toward the storm shelter behind the house, as they each carried the smaller children in their arms to the shelter. Their father was holding the storm shelter door open for the two children as they ran toward the door, but just as they were only a few steps away and it looked like they were going to make it, the tornado wind picked the two children up into the air, a little girl and her younger brother—just like you, Jerry and Louis. The two children were holding each other's hand tightly too as they ran, and continued to hold onto each other's hand as the wind picked them up. Their father and mother watched helplessly and in horror as the two children rose into the sky and began to spin as the tornado pulled them into its sinister whirling core. The children were found a little while later. The tornado had brought them down and blew them across a field directly into a barbed wire fence. It blew them with such force that the strands of barbed wire broke and rolled along with the two children, until they ended up in one massive ball of little boy, little girl, and a twisted, tangled mass of barbed wire—yet, you could see they still held each other's hands. They were in such a tangle it was impossible to separate the two children from the barbed wire, and so they were buried together, along with the barbed wire, in a common grave."

Louis and Jerry just sat there, eyes wide open and tears running down each of their cheeks as Aunt Betty finished her story. Everyone was silent for several moments. Finally, Grandma CC said, in a soft whisper to Jerry and Louis, still held firmly in her embrace, "If you ever find yourself caught outside in a tornado storm, you must lie down in a ditch or any low spot. Do not run away, it will catch you. If there is no low spot or ditch nearby, lie down near a tree or fence post, anything solidly planted in the ground, and just hold on with all your strength."

Roscoe went upstairs and left the house to go outside

and see what damage was done and help anyone who was in need, as everyone in the town emerged from whatever shelter they had and showed the same intentions.

Grandma CC took Louis and Jerry each by the hand and quietly said, "Off to bed with you two," as she quietly and gently dressed them in their pajamas, not saying anything. Louis was still thinking about the horror of the two children lost in the tornado. It sure got his attention. He was now terrified of tornados and what they could do. So was Jerry, who was also very quiet. As Louis and Jerry were ready for bed, Grandma CC said, "Now let us say our prayers...," and she knelt down bedside the bed, along beside Louis and Jerry, both also kneeling, and led them in prayer as they all said, "*Now I lay me down to sleep. I pray the Lord my soul to keep. If I should die before I wake, I pray the Lord my soul to take. And, Lord please bless our dear mother, Theresa, who lives with you in heaven now, along with our Grandpa Johannes.*"

In the instant they finished this prayer, a loud rumble of thunder shook the house! The storm was still making itself known, or perhaps this was a new storm rising over them. Louis and Jerry both let out a sharp scream! They rose from their knees and held tight to Grandma CC, who was still on her knees whispering her own silent prayers as only her lips moved, but no sound was heard. "There, there...it's okay, you two. That was just Saint Peter in heaven. He just spilled a wheelbarrow loaded with potatoes onto the great wooded floor in heaven. Sure makes a lot of noise!" As Grandma CC rose to her feet and lifted first Louis then Jerry into bed, snuggled them under the covers, and knowing their hearts

were still full of fear, she said, "You know when I am frightened at night and cannot sleep, I just put my hands together
in a prayer, with my thumbs crossed to form a Holy Cross,
then I say a little prayer to God to keep me safe, then I slide
my hands, still clasped together in prayer, under my cheek
and turn over on my side and close my eyes, knowing that
the Lord has sent my guardian angel to watch over each one
of us."

As Grandma CC spoke, Louis and Jerry each followed
the example of the story and folded their hands in prayer,
summoned their guardian angel to their side to watch over
them, and then with hands still clasped in prayer, placed
under their cheeks, they turned on their side and were soon
fast asleep.

This memory helped Louis pass the time as they
marched along the road, tired, starving, and wary of what
terror might happen next.

After a long day's march, Louis and the other POWs
could see they were approaching a large village with a train
station. There was a large crowd of French people standing
on the platform at the station. Along the track at the station
was a train with a long series of cattle cars connected. The
German guards began to squeeze the POW column into a
narrow, more ordered formation of four POWs abreast and
marched them right up onto the platform along the waiting cattle cars. As the column arrived and was ordered to
halt, the doors to the cattle cars were pulled open by railroad
workers and guards. The crowd of French people along the

platform began to push toward the cars too, and were very anxious—no, desperate—to board the train.

"Collaborators, anxious to leave France," Louis heard one guard say to another in German, which he was able to understand. A German officer ordered the group of guards on the right of the POWs to turn and face the crowd of French refugees. He then ordered them to fix their bayonets as they faced the crowd. The crowd kept pushing and probing for some way around the German troops and the POWs. They were desperate to reach the train. The officer ordered the German guards to fire once in the air over the French refugee's heads. This backed them off for only a moment, and then they continued to press forward. A second order was shouted out and the guards fired directly into the French refugees, many falling dead or wounded onto the platform. The refugee crowd scattered with screams of horror and frustration. Order restored, the German officer ordered the guards to herd the POWs into the train cars.

At first, Louis and the other prisoners greeted the sight of these trains with relief. Maybe now they got to ride to wherever they were being taken instead of marching all day on tired, blistered, and aching feet. All of the POWs were starving and weary from the long days of marching. They were exhausted from this, plus the constant threat of death from the guards, officers, or their own planes from the sky. But Louis and the others soon learned the train cars were to become a new form of unimaginable horror in themselves.

Louis and all the POWs were packed into the cattle cars so tightly that it was standing room only. There was not enough space to even squat to rest or relieve oneself. They were left packed in those rail cars for days at a time. It was to be their new home as the Germans moved them about the countryside. Many of the men had diarrhea. They were allowed out once a day to piss and eat. The Germans provided food that was usually a very weak soup, most often from a horse the Germans found and boiled in a great vat. The rest of the time the POWs were packed into the cattle cars. Men died of thirst. Men died of dysentery. Some men seemed to just go mad from the claustrophobia of being so tightly confined. The filth and stench was sickening. It was hell. Just amazing what a human can endure and what one human can do to another.

Other groups of prisoners were added to the boxcar train load, and as they were allowed off for food and personal relief, Louis recognized an officer from his regiment among the POWs. Louis approached him and introduced himself. The officer was in very bad shape and died later that evening from dysentery. But he told Louis what he had already heard before: that their regiment, the 507th regiment of the 82nd Airborne, unquestionably received the worst drop of the six US parachute regiments who jumped that first night of the invasion. Records reflect that the 507th parachute drop went horribly awry. Few, if any, troopers landed on assigned drop zones. Rather, they were scattered over an area approximately 15 miles on the north-south axis by 4 miles on the east-west axis, a rectangular box of about 60 square miles astride the Merderet River. Many were dropped even further out than this too.

Louis had been told by his sergeant, before he escaped, that their stick of paratroopers had landed near Valognes, which was about five miles northwest of their objective drop zone. This town was not even shown on their maps, it was so far from the targeted mission area.

Louis thought to himself, they had not trained for this eventuality, had not even considered it as a possibility. They were scattered so far and wide, nowhere near their drop zones. So many were captured, wounded, or killed. Many others died or drowned upon landing. One paratrooper was seen hanging from a church steeple that had snagged his parachute. He hung there for a long time during the early hours of the action. It took three days for the regiment to gather itself together as an organized tactical entity. And efforts were not helped when their regimental commander was captured on the second day after the invasion.

Louis found himself reviewing the past months in his mind, as he and so many others were prepared for their role in D-Day. At Alliance Army Airfield, Alliance, Nebraska, in late March the 507th co-located with Air Corp Troop Carrier forces in training. Rigorous advanced unit training to hone the collective skills of the regiment for combat was the daily order.

In late summer, it was put to the test in the field under the practiced eye of a 14-member team of examiners from the Airborne Command, and the 507th had won high marks, which garnered the entire regiment a vacation bivouac in the Black Hills of South Dakota. There were tactical jumps to test the defenses at distant airfields. They had some fun time too, Louis thought, for the troopers who volunteered for one of several jumps made in support of blood and bond drives in a four-state area. However, not all jumps went so well. Even during these practice jumps some paratroopers landed in ponds nearby and drowned accidentally. An outcome no one expected, but which would be a predictor of the fate awaiting many of the paratroopers who would later jump on D-Day and land in fields that had been flooded by the Germans, with just that result intended.

On the 28th of May, marshalling for the jump into Normandy began. The 1st Battalion moved to Fulbeck Airfield. There they were sealed into camp behind barbed wire fences. Security was at the maximum level. Terrain boards with miniature reproductions of the regimental objective area were used for repeated daily briefings of all soldiers. Actions to be taken upon landing; assembly and movement to assigned objectives were carefully gone over and reviewed repeatedly in every detail.

Neptune Operation was launched 5 June, but weather delayed it one day. As daylight on 5 June was drawing to a close, movement toward aircraft began. The 507th was ready and razor-sharp for action. At one minute before midnight, the trooper-laden C-47's roared into the air.

It took 117 aircraft to carry 2,004 troopers. The 507th PIR parachuted into Normandy to land on drop zone "T" shortly after 2:30 A.M., on the early morning of June 6, 1944. Their mission was to seize, organize, and defend its assigned area, clear the area within its sector, assist the 505th

PIR in securing the crossing of the Meredet River at La Fiere, then establish and maintain contact with the 508th PIR at Renouf and be prepared to advance to the west to the Douve River.

While not achieved as planned, the mission was accomplished despite extreme dispersion during the jump and very heavy combat casualties. As the heavily loaded C-47's crossed the Cotentin Peninsula coastline, a dense fog bank and German flak caused many planes to take evasive action and fly at excessive speed and altitudes not used in mass jumps. For example, most of HQ CO, 3rd Bat. landed in the town of Graignes, south of Carentan 16 miles away from their assigned drop zone.

Once on the ground, these courageous paratroopers were attacked by units of the veteran German 91st Division, on field maneuvers in the area. The German troops reacted promptly and laid down devastating fire on all the 82nd Airborne drop zones.

These conditions while crammed into the railroad boxcars were so dreadful that Louis found himself longing for the old days on the family farm where they at least had the use of an old outhouse to relieve themselves.... And Louis smiled to himself as he remembered the other use his dad made of their two-hole outhouse. Plus, if they got too filthy playing or working around the farm, they could always just jump in their big stock tank full of water for a quick and cleansing splash about.

But Louis could not think of the farm days without also

thinking of the steady flow of visitors in those days. All of them looking for the same thing, but not for the same reasons—they all wanted Dad's bootleg booze.

Then Louis' thoughts also returned to the day that preceded his and Jerry's return to the farm to live with their dad and the other brothers, Gene, Fred, and Marcel, plus their oldest sibling and sister, Martina. That was the day their beloved Grandma CC Pfeifer died....

In March 1929, Louis turned five. He was too young to fully understand the events that began to affect the adults in his life. But the tide of the prosperous 1920s had been turning for several years and the economic conditions were deteriorating fast. The weather had taken its toll on farmers' crops and income with the extreme droughts, frequent dust storms, then the plague of starving grasshoppers in swarms coming across the sky like a living dust storm, eating whatever was green and alive. If a farmer was fortunate enough to get a crop out of the ground during the drought, it seemed the stormy weather, wind, hail, and often just too much rain would destroy the crops. Business was in general decline, jobs were scarce, and unemployment was rising. Farm foreclosures were becoming commonplace, along with bank failures and closings.

People, many of them, were just becoming so desperate that some turned to crime. Gangsters and just common crooks roamed the land, and some became celebrated national heroes as bank robbers and bootleggers—to assault the very institutions the down-and-out folks blamed for their despair.

Then, in the last week of October 1929, starting on the 24th and up to the 29th, a day remembered as "Black Tuesday," the stock market collapsed. This took a devastating effect on so many thousands of people who did have money and invested it in the stock markets. It marked a turning point in American society from the era of the 1920s, which had been characterized by the virtues of self-reliance, self-confidence, and self-sufficiency, to a new era of social dependency. So many people who had always been able to make ends meet now found themselves on the "dole" and asking for a "handout" from others. The shame of accepting this help, plus the collapse of pride and the loss of personal dignity, took the national mood into a whirlwind of national depression—social and economic depression.

Grandma Cecelia was no exception to the times. She was an independent and self-sufficient woman, thanks in large part to her husband Johannes' prosperity during his lifetime. She also was an ardent and prudent investor. Her money was in stock, banks, and land. All was devastated by the collapse of the economy. The stress, heartache, and depression of the times took its toll on many, including Grandma Cecelia.

The summer of 1930 saw a long drought and unrelenting heat for day after day. The dust storms became regular events, filling the lungs of young and old alike with the terrible wind-driven dust. People and livestock alike, all were vulnerable to "dust-pneumonia" from breathing the dust-filled air, driven by high winds into every crack of door and window in people's homes.

Grandma Cecelia went into the hospital in August of that year. The unrelenting heat, dust-driven wind, and the stress and heartache of these times finally took their toll on her. Louis never forgot standing beside her hospital bed with his sister Jerry by his side. They were told to say their last goodbye to their Grandma CC. Jerry was crying, but Louis only felt a choking hurt in his throat and dread of the pending loss of the only mother he had really known so far in his short life. Grandma CC reached over with her hand and took first Jerry's, then added Louis' small hand to hers. She said to them both, "Do not be sad, my little sunny ones. I know what waits for me in heaven—more little angels just like you two. So, you both must always know and remember that even if I am gone, I am always with you and always love you each, as long as you remember me." Grandma CC passed away on August 20th. She was only 63 years old.

The very night she died, the area around Hays was inundated with soaking rains and a severe electrical storm. The storm included hailstones reported to be as much as two inches in diameter. The large hail damaged crops and was even reported to have killed chickens and birds in the trees.

The storm included a violent tornado that struck the area south of Hays and damaged a farm by picking up the big frame farmhouse and moving it three feet off its foundation. The roof and north side of the house was just blown away. Nearby, a barn was picked up by the tornado and set down intact about 100 yards away. A shed loaded with machinery was demolished and the equipment, along with a Ford Model T, was also found blown away nearly 100 yards from the farm. Fortunately, the family saw the storm coming and took refuge in their storm cellar, so no one was hurt.

But this family was friends and neighbors to the Pfeifer family, and it added to the grief and profound sense of loss on the day their beloved mother and grandmother Cecelia Pfeifer died. Louis remembered this funeral more vividly than his own mother's death. The great sadness and sense of loss were overwhelming to Louis and his sister Jerry…having once again, now lost the only woman in their lives they had known who gave them the unconditional love of family, parent, and mother—their Grandma CC.

Alex Pfeifer Family, ca. 1930
Back row, left to right
Eugene, Alex
Alfred, Martina, Marcel
Geraldine (Jerry) & Louis

Chapter 11

Back to the farm

After the death of Grandma Cecelia, in the terrible heat wave of August, 1930, Louis and Jerry returned to the family farm to rejoin their father, sister, and three older brothers. It was a big change in life for Louis and Jerry. Their time with Grandma was pampered city life compared to life on the farm. Plus, Grandma liked and kept a home of refinement consistent with her ample means in life. But life on the farm was greatly influenced by the many hardships of the times—and times were tough. Yet, their dad was good and generous to his kids, and that helped make up for the loss of affectionate nurturing from their grandma during the early days after the death of their mother, Theresa.

Their father, Alex, also managed to prosper fairly well for the times as a result of his ability to make and sell illegal liquor—in short, bootlegging. However, their dad never got into trouble for bootlegging. The revenue agents often came by and asked a lot of questions. They always drove really big cars, and had big guns too. And Louis admired their tall leather boots, since he was always barefoot in those days. They looked and acted dangerous. They were pretty serious people, those revenue men. One day they came by and pulled up to the house when Louis was the only one home. He was sick and did not have to go to school that day. One of the revenue men asked Louis if they had any whiskey today. He kept asking Louis questions. But Louis was well-schooled by his dad on the risks of bootleggers being caught, and he did not answer any questions. Louis just walked off into the house and left them sitting there in their big, fine car.

They got out of the car and started snooping around the farm. Louis just watched them from inside the house. They never bothered to look under the porch steps where Louis had just been sitting, so they did not find the jug of whiskey hidden there and waiting for the next customer to arrive.

One of the revenue men walked over to the chicken house and poked around in the gooseberry bushes growing beside the chicken house. Boy, you are so cold! Louis thought to himself as he watched from inside the house, thinking they were nowhere near finding the hidden whiskey…. Then Louis got worried! One of the revenue men walked over to the outhouse. He went inside and stayed long enough to relieve himself, and then walked out and continued snooping around. Louis held his breath and felt his heart pounding as the revenue agent was inside the outhouse. Little did the man know that he was sitting on top of Dad's secret stash of whiskey, hidden in a jug, wrapped in a towel, tucked inside a boxed compartment just under the two-hole seat in the outhouse. A pair of hidden hinges enabled Dad to just walk out there and lift the two-hole seat and pull out a gallon jug wrapped in a towel to protect it, and take care of any legitimate customer that came by needing their supply of homemade whiskey.

That was some childhood during those days. Once the agents even tried an airplane! It flew over the farm and circled several times. Then they must have spotted the still out in an area of the cornfield. They flew over the ridge and seemed to be coming back to land along the road, but it was too hilly, so they had to land a couple of miles away and walk back to the farm. But by then Gene and Fred had taken the still down and hidden it in a dug-out cave that was concealed in the cornfield. The cave was where the large barrels of corn mash were stored. The revenue agents finally arrived and walked into the cornfield. They were in there for a long time. They might have even gotten lost for a while. Finally they came back out. They had found nothing and were pretty mad. All the kids had made themselves scarce and could not be found either. Eventually the agents left, and the last Louis saw of them was as they walked down the road in the same direction they came from, where they'd left their airplane. Soon he heard the airplane take off and those agents buzzed the farm several times before they left. That was fun to watch. But they never tried an airplane again to find the still on the farm.

Louis remembered the first time he took a drink of Dad's whiskey—it was Marcel's idea. He had dared Louis to sneak a taste, so he decided to try the whiskey for himself that one day. Louis got so drunk on a small glass of it that he could not walk right. He just staggered around and kept falling down. Fred thought it was so funny, he could not stop laughing. He took a few sips too and kept offering Louis more. He was always a lot of help in those situations, Louis remembered to himself with a slight smile.

Then Jerry came outside and scolded Louis for being so silly and getting his clean coveralls so dirty. So, in appreciation of Jerry's criticism, Louis told her he would get her muddy too and started chasing her around the barnyard. He soon caught Jerry, and even though he was younger, he was strong, and he picked Jerry up and heaved her over the fence into the pigpen. Jerry was kicking and screaming every moment! The pigs just scattered in snorts and protests.

Fred and Marcel were watching from around the corner of the house. But Louis and Jerry could hear them laughing hysterically. Then, because Louis loved his big sister too and he felt so guilty, he climbed over the fence and jumped into the pigpen too, just to help Jerry to her feet. She was so muddy and smelly! Jerry was not at all happy about this, but soon saw the humor in the situation too—Louis was just feeling no pain and still in the grips of Dad's homemade booze. So, Jerry and he decided to clean themselves up by taking a swim in the big stock tank.

Little did they know that Marcel and Fred, the Knopke boys, as Jerry and Louis called them, were still watching from around the corner. "Knopke" in German meant essentially the "hired hands," which implied the three older brothers were really nothing more than employees, and certainly did not share their status as "family" members.

Well, Marcel spotted a three-foot-long black snake moving in the grass along the fence and within a moment caught it, then came running around the house swinging the big snake over his head and tossed it into the stock tank where

Jerry and Louis were splashing around. Both of them feared snakes more than anything, and they screamed in unison! Then they climbed out of the stock tank and ran into the house as fast as their bare feet could carry them, screaming and yelling with each step. Louis and Jerry could still hear Marcel and Fred laughing outside for a long time. They really enjoyed that antic, and later, when Louis and Jerry had recovered from the horror of swimming with a snake that was as long as they were tall, they got a big laugh out of it too.

There was a steady stream of customers coming by the farm for Dad's booze in those days. The Pfeifer farm set on very high ground. They could see visitors coming long before they got to the front drive, so they always knew who was approaching and if they were safe or not. During the colder months, Dad would set up the still right in the kitchen of the house. It was amazing he never got caught!

Old Lady McGuire, a very big woman who had a driver and drove a really big Buick, would come out to the farm for her booze regularly. She would pull up and stick her head out the window and yell, "Alex Pfeifer! Got any 'lickker' today?" Dad would always come over and chat with her while one of the boys would fill up her back seat with jugs of booze.

Most customers never came near the house to make a pickup. They were much more careful. Each of those customers had a stone fence post assigned to them. It was at the base of that fence post, hidden by weeds and overgrowth, that Dad would hide their bottle of booze. They would drive by and just stop and pick it up, often after dark, and stayed clear of the farm in case it was being watched by the revenue agents. Dad's bootlegging went on for a long time and kept the family going during the Depression. Dad would charge $8 a gallon for his booze. Dad always had money in his pocket and friends in those days, but he had many enemies too.

The bootleg booze started with cooked wheat mash. Sometimes they had three or four huge barrels of mash going, and one of the boys had to watch it, usually Fred, for days at a time. The mash was cooked to a point that it released vapors of pure grain alcohol, which became liquid as it cooled in the coils over the still. The grain alcohol then dripped into the jugs. On a good day they would average about one gallon per day. It was clear and potent, if not downright volatile. They cut it with water, then colored and flavored the distilled alcohol with burnt sugar. Dad gave away as much as he sold, to keep certain friends happy, maybe pay some debts, or help those who had helped him. It was as good as real currency in those days. But they were constantly moving the still too, so it would not be found. There were also two dug-out caves in the field to hide the barrels and the still when necessary. The used mash was fed to the chickens and pigs.

Dad was sad a lot during those days. Often in the evening, he would just sit on the front porch and stare off into space. Louis always imagined he was missing Mom. But Dad never talked about her or the night she died. She was pregnant when she was lost. Dad was snow-blind for about one year after that night, and his vision very slowly returned.

His eyelashes and eyebrow hair froze off too, but it eventually grew back. He had permanent damage to his sight in one eye due to the snow-blinding damage.

Dad was often just sleeping on the divan in the living room. Once Marcel and Louis got into a big argument and Louis started cussing Marcel out. Louis was just saying every swearword he knew. Well, Dad would often ask Louis to stuff tobacco in his pipe, and when he needed Louis for that he would softly say, "Louis, come here, son…." Just as Louis finished swearing at Marcel, Louis heard Dad's voice in the old soft manner say, "Louis, come here, son." Louis did not even know his dad was awake. So, despite Louis' anger and fighting with Marcel, he immediately walked across the room to see what his dad wanted. When he got within one step of Dad, without rising from his prone position on the divan, he slapped Louis across the face so hard it knocked him across the room, and he fell backwards onto his butt. Dad then said in that same even, soft voice, "Louis, never let me hear you swear like that again." The next thing Louis heard was Marcel laughing as he ran out of the living room, through the kitchen, and out the back door—lest he would be the next one summoned to Dad's side.

Louis just sat there, feeling hurt from the slap, and his gullibility for walking right over to his dad to receive it. Then Louis' anger at Marcel returned for setting him up for this punishment in the first place. But Marcel was nowhere to be found, naturally.

A few days later, Louis saved Marcel's life. Dad went to town, and Martina was home to keep an eye on things, including the kids. The chickens had gotten into a really huge haystack in the barnyard and just spread it all over the place. So Dad told Marcel to take the fork and rake and get that mess of hay back up into a pile. It was a really big stack of hay. And he said Louis could help. So he had no more than got out of sight when Marcel said, "Louis, I'll go hitch up a team of horses and we'll hook up the hay-rake and rake it up, it will be a lot faster."

No sooner were the horses harnessed and hooked to the tongue of the hay rake than something spooked them! The two workhorses jumped forward in one mighty lurch, then took off running full gallop!

Maybe it was a horsefly bite or a hornet sting…. Well, where the horses' harnesses are hooked up to the tongue of the hay-rake, it suddenly broke in the back when it connected to the hay-rake axle—with a big jerk! Man those horses took off and everything followed: harness, hay-rake, and Marcel. The sudden lurch forward of the horses threw Marcel back against the seat, then forward again as the horses went into a full galloping stride. As he went forward, Marcel fell off the hay-rake seat and to the ground in front of the hay-rake and the horses' pounding hoofs.

The hay-rake had a lever that controlled the hay-rake in the up and down position. They took off so fast—the horses ran a full gallop as fast as they could go, pulling the hay-rake behind them, with Marcel rolling along under the sharp-pointed tongs of the hay-rake! The school was catty-corner across from the barnyard, and they ran in that direction down the hill. The ground was rough and it was very stony. Marcel had fallen down within the rake wearing his new overalls made of very tough denim material, so there he was just bouncing and tumbling over and over and around inside that hay-rake. Louis gave chase too, running after the horses and hay-rake as fast as he could in his bare feet over the rough rocky ground. The horses finally ran over to the fence corner and came to a stop. Louis just came up to them, slowly and carefully, and took the reins. He did not want to spook them again with Marcel lying underneath all the sharp spring steel teeth of the hay-rake. Louis was really scared. Then he tied the horses' long leather reins to a stone fence post to keep them from taking off again.

Marcel was still conscious, and in spite of his wounds and injuries, he was concerned for his younger brother Louis' safety too. He told Louis not to get in front of the horses in case they took off again. So, Louis carefully unhooked the horses from the harness and broken tongue of the hay-rake and helped Marcel get out from within the hay-rake. He managed to stagger up to the garage near the house. His new overalls were shredded and twisted all around him, like a figure eight.

Marcel was cut, scratched, scraped, bruised, and bleeding all over. Still, he was more worried about the horses and told Louis to go get them and take them back to the barn first. Louis got the horses in the barn and went to help Marcel, who was hiding in the garage. He then told Louis to go in and get a bucket of water and to not tell anybody. Well, Martina was the only one home. So, Louis got the soap, water, a tub, towels, clean clothes, and Martina never saw him nor asked any questions. So, there Marcel was, shaking and shivering, a total mess—and yet, they were not going to tell anyone.

But what were they really thinking? Not tell anyone? The straw was still scattered all over the barnyard, the hay-rake now had a broken tongue. It was leaning up against the fence just across the lane and was just a pile of wreckage, and the horses were sweating in the stalls in the barn, but the two boys didn't know anything. Not to mention Marcel's bloodied new coveralls all ruined and having been new just that morning, plus his bloody, cut, bruised, and scraped body. This would be their secret, right? That is family, and looking out for each other—as they learned, always.

Marcel was so full of stickers and cuts from rocks, it was unbelievable. He was running a fever the next day, and Dad took him to the doctor. Dad never even got mad. He just dealt with the whole thing in stride. Dad was generally pretty good to all the kids. Given the times, the Depression, and being a single dad, he took fairly good care of his family.

Louis was getting kind of macho in those days. Sort of full of himself, and Marcel liked to tease him, which always got Louis very agitated. So one day Louis knew Dad was going away again the next day, and Louis told Marcel that Dad was going to leave tomorrow and when he did leave, "I am going to take you out there and beat the daylights out of you!"

Next day, Dad left and Marcel said, "Well Jake (he never called Louis by his real name), Dad is gone." Just to remind Louis of his promise to beat the crap out of him next time

Dad was gone. And Louis said, "Yeah, I know that…," but nothing happened. Marcel was much older and bigger than Louis, and huskier too. Well, Louis had learned making a threat was one thing; following up was still another.

The next older brother to Marcel was Fred. He was a twin, but his other twin died shortly after childbirth. Fred was always the enterprising one in the family. Guess he just took after Dad and always knew a way to make a buck or two. One day in town, Louis saw Fred walking down the street with a gunnysack, or burlap bag, full of something. Louis stopped Fred and asked him what he was doing and what he had in the gunnysack. Fred said it was full of chicken heads from the butcher shop, plus coal dust from Grandma Pfeifer's furnace. He opened the bag for Louis to look inside. All Louis saw was about two dozen disgusting and smelly black chicken heads chopped from their bodies. Fred relieved Louis' bewilderment as to why anyone would want a sack full of black chicken heads by explaining, "The county will pay a bounty on dead crows of ten cents each. But the heads are so smelly and disgusting that they hardly ever look in the bag or even count them. They just take my word for what's inside," Fred said, grinning his biggest smile, all teeth showing. "It is the easiest $2.40 you can get in this town," Fred added, as he turned and headed off on his mission to collect his bounty.

All the Pfeifer kids had nicknames, but some were not very nice. Such as when Jerry and Louis called their three older brothers the "Knopke boys." "Knopke" was German for "hired help," implying the older boys were not really "family" to Louis and Jerry.

Jerry and Louis had their own special language and code words. For example, they each had these old iron wagon wheel rims they played with as if they were cars. Louis and Jerry would get them rolling along, then guide or steer them with a sturdy stick. Then they would roll their wheels up beside each other and one would ask the other, "Well, have you seen those Knopke boys around here today?" The other would say, "No, and I sure hope I don't 'cause they can be very ornery!" Great fun when you are only six or seven years old. Jerry and Louis got along famously, a very close relationship as brother and sister goes. She was the only true friend Louis ever had as a child, or for the rest of his life, as it turned out. Jerry never loved anyone more than her brother Louis and always considered it her duty to look out for her younger brother, just as her mother and grandmother would have wanted her to do.

But living on the farm with Dad and Martina and the rest of the family was not all child's play. The Depression was real and times were very hard. Plus, the occasional dust storm would blow up just to remind you that no matter how bad it was, it could always get worse. A Kansas dust storm was an unbelievable event. Usually in the afternoon, around two or three o'clock, it would get still—very, very still.

In the Kansas prairie, the wind seems to never stop blowing. So, when it does become still, and the wind stops…that is the time to start worrying. Everyone would turn their eyes to the sky and examine the clouds to see what was brewing. Then the wind would pick up and before you knew it, a black wall cloud of dust would come rolling across the prairie. The cloud would be so high into the sky it would block out the sun. The black cloud brought dust that would drift just like snow. Deep ditches would fill up level with the ground with dust. During these terrible wind and dust storms, the electricity nearly always went out too.

People tried to keep the black dust out of their homes by nailing sheets over their windows, but it always found a way inside. Cattle, chickens, and other animals would die in the pastures due to breathing the dust-laden air. People got very sick too; some even died. It was a hellish time, and took a toll on farmers and everyone else too. It would get dark, very dark, just as the times were also so dark.

Chapter 12

Stalag 4D – welcome to hell

"Jude! Sie jüdisch?" Louis heard an officer yell in his face as the line was formed in the new POW camp the first morning for roll call. Louis, understanding the German, knew he'd asked him, "Jew! You...Jewish?"

That was the first thing Louis heard from this guard officer when his group of POWs had finally arrived at their work camp—Stalag 4D. The officer took one look at Louis and his big nose and determined that he looked decidedly Jewish. This singled Louis out for a special interrogation.

Louis was taken by two guards into one of the buildings the German officers used to run the camp. He was walked into an office with another SS officer in the usual black uniform sitting behind a desk.

"Sitzen Sie sich hin," the officer said in a tone that clearly was not a request.

"Sit down" was understood by Louis immediately, but he continued to stand, in his ruse to not reveal that he could speak German. It was just too useful and important to be able to overhear Germans talking without knowing they were being understood. Louis just stood there staring straight at the SS officer with the poker face he had long since mastered.

"Nehmen Sie einen Sitzjuden!" the SS officer demanded

in a shout.

"Take a seat, Jew!" was understood by Louis, and the officer was clearly making it an order and not a request. Louis allowed some degree of panic to be revealed in his eyes and manner, to only let the officer know that the anger in his voice was being understood, if not the orders.

The SS officer glared at one of the guards and with his eyes motioned to the chair, and the guard jammed his rifle butt into Louis' back hard enough to knock him down into the chair and almost onto the floor. Louis put himself on to the chair, carefully, with apprehension, and not taking his eyes off the SS officer. But Louis was also careful not to show defiance, so he would not further antagonize this officer either. Louis understood the officer was asking if he was Jewish, and it was a thin line to deny this… it could result in the same response either way—instant death, or removal to the death camps he had recently heard of….

The SS officer lit a cigarette and looked a little relaxed for a moment. Then he did something Louis did not expect. The SS officer held the cigarette out toward Louis as if to offer him a smoke too. Louis only turned his head back and forth to say, "No." The officer sat there in silence, puffing on his cigarette and staring at Louis, just waiting, waiting perhaps for Louis to say something? Louis did not know what the officer was really up to; he just realized this was a life or death situation for him to endure.

Suddenly the SS officer stood up, pulled his Lugar pistol from its holster as he rushed around the desk and pointed the Lugar at Louis' forehead, the end of the barrel pressed hard against his forehead. He cocked the pistol and said, "Schmutzige stinkende Ratte stellte Juden...gegenüber!"

"Dirty, stinking, rat-faced Jew...!" Louis thought to himself as he understood the German—even with a German Lugar pistol jammed against his forehead and death maybe eminent, Louis could not help thinking, who's calling who a "rat face"? Yet Louis, not taking his eyes off the officer, felt the impulse that death was at hand and said nothing. Louis could feel the sweat running down the side of his face and the small of his back, as the natural fear of death made his body react.

However, strangely, he did not feel fear either. Instead, Louis thought of his mother and what she'd endured in her long night of terror as she froze to death. At least my death will be sudden and quick, he thought, as all this and more flashed in an instant before his mind's eye... maybe Mom and Grandma CC are waiting for me now, on the other side...and I will be with them in just another instant... that really sounds better than this place.... Louis felt an impulse to actually smile in defiance and the absurdity of his thoughts given the dire circumstances of the moment, but he controlled his impulse to smile, knowing the officer would see it as a mocking gesture and surely pull the trigger. Louis also felt a growing confidence in this instant of his readiness for sudden death and his ability to control his thoughts and reactions in spite of it...!

"Jüdischer bastard!"

Louis' mind provided the instant translation: "JEWISH BASTARD!" The officer shouted this so loud even the two guards flinched as he again pushed the pistol so hard against Louis forehead, it nearly knocked him off his chair. Still, without moving his eyes from the eyes of the commandant, and without blinking, Louis said, "Catholic."

"Lügner!"

"LIAR!"—again the instant translation in Louis' mind. Louis considered himself already dead, and found these words softly, quietly coming out of his mouth:

"Hail Mary, full of grace, the Lord is with thee, blessed art thou amongst women and blessed is the fruit of thy womb, Jesus. Holy Mary, Mother of God, pray for us sinners, now and at the hour of our death...AMEN."

Louis saw moisture building in the SS officer's eyes. The white of his eyes was turning slightly red. He was responding in a way Louis did not expect, although he had no idea what to expect.

The SS officer slowly softened the pressure of the pistol barrel against Louis' forehead, then lowered the pistol very slowly and turned his back on Louis. He said nothing as he stepped back around his desk and then sunk down into his chair. He very slowly lit yet another cigarette, while the first cigarette was still smoking in the ashtray on the desk. He gestured with his hand to the guard to take Louis away... as Louis left the room, he was sure he could hear the SS officer say in a soft whisper, *"Hail Holy Queen, Mother of Mercy, our life, our sweetness, and our hope... To thee we do cry, poor banished Children of Eve, to thee we send up our sighs mourning, and weeping in this veil of tears*"—in perfect English.

As Louis left the SS officer's office, escorted by the two guards through the door, one guard whispered in English, very softly to Louis so no one could hear, "Catholic," and nodded back toward the SS officer.

Then the guard winked at Louis and smiled. Louis looked at him, and very slightly smiled back as the whisper left his lips too, and he and the guard pointed at each other saying ever so quietly, "*Catholic.*"

Louis nearly collapsed into his bunk when he was finally marched back to the POW barracks. He was soaked with sweat, plus mentally and physically exhausted from the ordeal of the encounter with this officer. Louis felt himself sinking into the depths of despair and depression. He wondered what he did to deserve the life he found himself living. Why him? He imagined just making a break for the fence around the POW barracks, with the virtually certain outcome of a sudden end to this life that seemed to follow each miserable moment by another, then another....

Then, in the darkness, Louis heard the familiar sound he heard each night. The low rumble of bombers approaching in the distance. Another night of terror coming in for all POWs, and Germans, soldiers, and civilians, as never-ending bombing heaped death and destruction upon them. Louis, lying there in the darkness thinking that death might be a blessing at this point, remembered another terrible day when the darkness descended on the farm and the distant rumble of thunder filled the sky....

Chapter 13

Windmills, tornados, and a runaway too

Late in November 1930, it had been a night warmer than usual for that time of year, and the sunrise was greeted by a thick overcast of dark brooding clouds. By mid-morning, the sky was black with heavy clouds beginning to swirl as air currents pushed them in variable directions. Alex, and his oldest son Gene, had finished doing the chores of feeding the livestock and putting them inside the barn for shelter. As they walked back to the house, the wind turned very cold and picked up to a fierce, sudden blow. One last chore remained—to put the windmill vane into neutral to stop the windmill turning so fast in the coming storm. Otherwise, the windmill could just blow itself apart. Gene got to the windmill first and pushed down on the lever with the guy-wire attached to the chain at the top that would disengage the vane on the back of the windmill. But the cable snapped! The strain of the cold wind, and perhaps the age of the cable—whatever, it snapped...now the only way to save the windmill from certain destruction was to climb up the windmill and pull the chain by hand.

Alex arrived at the windmill at the same moment, and with a quick glance at the situation told Gene, "Get up there and pull that damn chain before the windmill blows itself into pieces!"

Gene was a strong and independent person. He had turned 15 years old that past August and was already resisting his dad's authority. That was the main reason he and his dad did not get along at all as he got older. In fact, a turning point in his life was to be this horrible windy day the windmill tried to tear itself apart. Gene was no coward. But any fool could see that the wind alone could blow a person off that windmill as he climbed the spindly ladder up the side. Plus, in the roaring wind it looked like the windmill would just fall over at any moment, with the windmill fan and blades already spinning at maximum speed!

Just then a fierce bolt of lightning struck the ridge less than a quarter mile away! The instant flash was followed by a crack of thunder that in itself felt like it could knock a person off their feet.

The fierce storm was blowing in fast from the southwest, and the sky turned from black to a sickening greenish black. The clouds were rolling in fast as the squall line formed across the sky. The wind was just furious and made it very hard to even walk without something to hold onto.

The wire-cable from the control lever at the bottom of the windmill to the chain-switch to throw the windmill rudder into neutral had broken. So the neutral switch to throw the windmill fan into a stable neutral drive could not be engaged. The fan was spinning so fast the entire tower was vibrating and shuttering. Even the ground under the windmill seemed to shake with the commotion.

Alex, who was now holding onto the windmill to keep

from being blow away, told Gene again to climb up to the top of that windmill and manually put the damn chain control into neutral, then reinstall the broken wire-cable on the chain.

Gene said, "No." Clearly it was very dangerous. Plus the wind was so fierce it might just blow over the entire windmill with Gene hanging on. There was little or nothing to hang onto as one climbed a windmill, and the further up you went the more top-heavy and unstable the whole rig would be. Plus, the highest point around for miles was that windmill and clearly the most likely place lightning might strike next. Gene considered the risk, to himself or his dad, but saving the windmill from destruction just did not seem to be worth his life, or his dad's. Plus, his sense of self-preservation overruled any other thoughts...including obedience to his father's commands.

Then his dad threatened Gene with a beating he would never forget if he did not do as he was told. Gene just turned his back and walked off the farm and down the road, never to return to the farm again. Gene was leaning into the fierce wind as he walked, and soon a deluge of rain came pouring down.

Louis was home from school sick, as he often was in his younger days. He and Martina were watching the drama unfold from the kitchen window. Louis recalled how bad he felt for Gene—to leave home on a day like this and then to make that long walk into town, or wherever he was going. One thing for sure, there was no shelter for miles in all directions from their farm.

Alex did climb the windmill in this fierce wind and pulled the chain to set the spinning windmill into neutral. He came into the house soaking wet. He did not say a word to anyone. The house was dark because the power lines were blown down. He set about lighting several kerosene lanterns. He asked Martina to put lunch on the table for Louis, her and himself. Martina and Louis both felt frightened of their dad's anger…but he actually seemed calm and was very quiet.

As soon as lunch was eaten and the storm had died down, Alex told Louis to get his coat on, they were going for a ride. He told Martina to stay home and wait for the rest of the kids to come home from school.

Alex Pfeifer did not say anything to Louis, but Louis imagined his dad was going down the road to search for and find the runaway, Gene. Louis knew very well that his dad could be calm and cool on the outside and raging mad inside without giving anyone a clue to his true feelings. Alex had a reputation for being an astute poker player and Louis already understood that not showing your feelings was a key to that talent, as well as so many other things in life. Louis felt very worried for Gene if he was found by his Dad—he was in for the lickin' of his life!

They had no sooner pulled out onto the gravel road when the neighbor came driving up the road and hailed Alex to stop. He said to Alex that he had just been in town and heard a tornado had hit the school where Alex's nephew Herbert Pfeifer was the teacher. Herbert was the 24-year-old son of Alex's brother, Anton Pfeifer. The school sat north of

Victoria, just a few miles east of Hays. The neighbor told Alex the storm that just passed had rained nearly two inches of rain in less than two hours. There was apparently considerable damage along the path of a tornado that passed between Hays and Victoria, a few miles south of the Alex Pfeifer farm. "They need help over there for sure," the neighbor told Alex. He was going home to get his wife, then head over to the school himself.

Alex drove as fast as the muddy, rut-filled, gravel road would allow to the school. Along the way there was no sign of his son Gene. Clearly, Alex was worried, and so was little six-year-old Louis… did the tornado get his big brother Gene too?

When Alex and Louis arrived to the place where the school once sat, there was nothing left. Only a splintered pile of debris strewed across the field toward the southeast for a great distance. Only the old stone foundation and the floor of the school building remained to show where the school was once.

Alex surveyed the debris in the field and the direction the wind had carried the splintered remains of the wood-frame school building. He could see the tornado came from the general direction that would lead back to his own farm. He thought how grateful and fortunate he was that it was not the school that sat at the corner of his own farm, where his children and the neighbors were taught. Not to mention the chance that this tornado could have hit his own farm too. Then, he remembered his son Gene, who was last seen walking down the road toward town, about the same time this tornado was forming. Alex said a silent prayer that Gene was all right; Louis saw his dad silently do the sign of the cross… Louis understood he was praying. Louis crossed himself and folded his hands together in prayer too.

Louis was already terrified of tornados and the fierce storms of the Kansas plains, but seeing this destruction firsthand left him with a formidable dread of tornados and the loud roar that announced them to the poor souls in their path.

Herbert and many of the children suffered minor injuries, but no one was missing or killed. Several people had already arrived before Alex and Louis. Alex and Louis found one of the neighbors putting bandages on Herbert's injuries as he explained what had happened. The storm hit them without any warning, he said. They heard it about the same moment the building began to disintegrate. He ordered the kids outside and to lie down in the nearest ditch for shelter.

This was not the first time Gene and his dad had a showdown over something like this, but in Gene's mind, it was clearly going to be the last. Gene found shelter in town someplace and just knocked around town after that day. Once in a while Louis and the other kids would see Gene slip into the barn late in the evening, when he would come home because he had no place else to stay. Louis helped Martina sneak food to him too. But none of the kids ever saw any of that happen—as far as their dad was concerned. It was their secret from their dad. Martina would make sure Dad never knew. But Gene never showed his face around the farm again whenever his dad was around.

Louis finally fell asleep in his bunk, in the POW barracks, as he blocked out the sound of the allied bombers overhead and the distant concussions and blasts of the bombs they dropped. The memory of that terrible storm and the day Gene ran away helped Louis take his mind somewhere else. He thought about his older brother Gene. How young he was when he struck out on his own. Louis thought about the hardships his oldest brother must have endured. He was so proud of him, and the kind of person he grew up to be. Louis felt his great love and admiration for Gene, who had done so much for Louis and his other brothers. Louis resolved that he too was just as strong and tough, and vowed that he would make his oldest brother proud of him too.

Chapter 14

Time to grow up fast

I t was November 1930, and Gene was only 15 years old. Times were very tough in Hays to be out on your own. The Depression was in full bloom and jobs were very scarce. Plus farmers were having a horrible time with drought, dust storms, bad markets, and if they did get a decent crop coming in, the starving bugs or jackrabbits would eat their fill and destroy most of the crop. It seemed the only people who had any money were the bootleggers—which of course included their dad, Alex.

Gene could have taken refuge at his Grandma Cecelia Pfeifer's home when he ran away from the farm. But she had passed away just a few months before. Plus, if she were still living, that would have been the first place his dad would have looked for him. Yet, Gene was well liked and many respected him for leaving home. Many of these were the same folks who disliked his father, and knew or feared his well-known, ill-tempered ways. So, Gene found shelter and friends wherever he could, but it was tough—the times were tough for everyone. Odd jobs to earn a meal were scarce, and many drifters and out-of-work, down-on-their-luck men roamed every small town in the country.

Many people turned to crime to survive, and gangs of criminals roamed the land from coast to coast. Bank robbers, highway robbers, gamblers, and thieves just went from town to town to make a living by stealing from anyone with a few bucks in their pockets. Gene learned this the hard way not long after he left home. It even made the newspaper in Hays.

It was October 1931, and Gene had gone to Hutchinson with his friend George Weber, and they were on their way home to Hays on a cold, foggy morning. They stopped for breakfast along the way at a café in Lyons. Moments after they arrived, two well-dressed strangers also entered the café and invited themselves to join Gene and George at their table. One was about 30 years old and the other was a little younger. But they seemed to be friendly and agreeable sort of men. A pleasant conversation ensued among the four men as they ate their breakfast.

Later, Gene and George would remember that the Ford the two men traveled in had been following them all the way from Hutchinson. So, during the breakfast, another customer asked George if he could change a $10 bill. He obliged and in doing so, revealed that he had more money than that in his pocket.

Well, as they finished their breakfast, Gene and George continued down the highway to Hays. About one mile out of Lyons, the other two men in the Ford, still following Gene and George, caught up with them, and after hailing them to pull over they asked for help from George to fix a broken windshield wiper on their car. It had been revealed by George Weber that he worked at Fellers Motor Company in Hays. Being an agreeable sort, Weber got out of his car to see what he could do to help with the Ford wiper. He'd no sooner discovered there was nothing wrong with the wiper than he felt an automatic revolver pressed into his back, and the two men demanded his money. George Weber gave the men all he had, which was only $11, and then they took all Gene had too, which was only $9. As Gene and George stood there with their pockets turned inside out and empty, they watched the two well-dressed men drive off in their Ford. Gene, who worked for Hoch Laundry in Hays at the time, said it would take him a while to save up another $9… but at least they still had enough gas left in their car to make it home to Hays.

Chapter 15

Buckets of blood

Martina, Louis' oldest sister, and he had a thing going that they loved to do. She would work very late making bread for the family and keep little Louis up late too churning butter. So, when the bread came out of the oven, all fresh and warm, a scent that you never forget—with fresh butter melted on that hot bread, plus maybe some sugar too—Martina and Louis just sat down and made a nice meal of this treat in the middle of the night. On one of those nights, well after Louis had gone to bed and was supposed to be asleep, he could still hear Martina working in the kitchen cleaning up.

Yet, perhaps she was also waiting for their dad to come home. He had gone to town as he often did and would drink and gamble with some of his friends. Well, on this night, it was now about four years after Mom had died, yet Dad was still suffering from some of the snow-blindness damage to his vision and still could be pretty depressed about the loss of Mom. Dad came in very late, or actually very early in the morning. Dad often met his friends in town for drinking and poker or craps games. He just staggered into the house. Louis could hear him. He heard Martina go to the door to help him stagger over the threshold. "Dad, what happened to you…?" Louis heard Martina ask in a very hushed whisper. "Damn bastards...," he heard Dad mumble in a drunken slur.

Louis could not just lie there and listen. His curiosity got the best of him and he silently got out of bed without waking up his brothers, who all slept in the same bed at that time. Louis peeked outside the door into the living room. Martina was helping Dad lie down on the divan in the living room. It looked like he was really beaten up. Both his eyes were swollen shut, and his lips were split open and he was bleeding from his nose and mouth. Louis could see he had taken a real beating.

Martina quietly walked into the kitchen with some haste and prepared a pan of water. Then she returned and sat on the sofa against her dad's side. She slowly and gently began to blot the caked blood from Dad's face. Dad's speech was slurred and he was very drunk. He was mumbling curse words quietly to those who had jumped him and beaten him so severely...something about blaming him for the death of his wife, and this would give him what he deserved. Minutes passed as Martina was nearly finished washing the blood off his face. Louis then saw that their dad was becoming very quiet.

Then Louis heard Dad say, in a slurred whisper, "Oh Theresa, I loved you so, how could you leave us...?" He opened his swollen eyes just slightly as he said it and was looking straight into Martina's eyes.

Martina said, "Dad, it's me, Martina, Mom is dead—remember?" as a tear went down her cheek. Then Dad reached up with his arm and pulled Martina down on top of him and kissed her mouth; she pushed back and tried to get away, but quietly, still afraid to wake the whole house. Her struggle did not help, and within a moment of the first kiss, Dad pulled Martina even closer and rolled over on top of her. Louis did not understand what was happening, but felt afraid to watch any longer. He was so afraid of his dad in this condition that he did not want to get caught out of bed watching him and Martina. Louis quietly went back to bed as he heard Martina's muffled pleas to her father to please stop. Louis found himself wondering if this was the first time, or had this been going on for a while?

Louis had lots of compassion for his dad. He never really wanted to believe what people said their dad did to his oldest sister, Martina. Louis was only ten when it all began to come out in the papers in 1934, and the terrible results happened to Louis and the entire family. Yet, just a few years later, after Martina turned 18 and left home, she would accuse Dad of doing very bad things to her. The story was in the newspapers, and the sheriff who arrested him, and most folks in town, just assumed he must be guilty.

But Louis did remember once seeing buckets of blood, or at least it was very bloody water. It was by accident, and he was not supposed to come into the house. A doctor had come over to the home from the adjoining town just to help keep things quiet. Martina was not well, especially in the morning when she woke up nauseated. So she was in the big bedroom, in bed, just moaning…covered with a white sheet as the doctor bent over working on her. Louis felt so bad for her. He saw the doctor's helper bring buckets full of bloody water out of that room several times. Louis did not know or understand what was going on in there…and he did not want to know. Louis was very young, but not just naïve; he grew up on a farm and understood a lot for his age. He was very afraid of what might happen next to his family.

Martina only went out with a boyfriend once while she lived at the farm, and her dad put a quick stop to that. He had become very watchful and possessive of Martina and how, and with whom, she spent her time. He rarely allowed her to be alone and kept a close eye on her all the time. Even the kids realized things were different now with Martina and their dad. She seemed more like the house-mother, in their mother's absence. Jerry and Louis, the youngest, did not fully understand what was going on…but Gene, the oldest brother, seemed to know, and his relations with his dad had grown more and more tenuous, until Gene finally just ran off on that terrible stormy day.

Alex had a reputation in town. He was not well liked. He was tough and fast to use his fists to settle a quarrel, even for those times. He would flatten a person out on the ground real quick. He had a lot of enemies, and many people despised him. They were also very jealous of him too. He was successful. He always had money. He was very good looking, and as many women loved him as men or women hated him. So, when the troubles came, his enemies made themselves known in great numbers.

Chapter 16

Father is accused

1934 was a very dark time in Louis' life and for many others too. The United States and the world were still in the grips of a grim depression. President Franklin Roosevelt was just starting the second year of his first presidency, presiding over a nation with 13,000,000 people unemployed. Bank failures were rampant. But, on the most personal level, foreclosures of farms and homes in great numbers tore at the very fabric of society.

Yet, darker clouds than anyone fully understood at the time were gathering in Europe too. Benito Mussolini, the Fascist dictator of Italy, was meeting with the newly elected Adolph Hitler, another Fascist in Germany, who had just won 95.7% of the German people's vote.

Meanwhile, across the Midwest, drought prevailed and massive dust storms continued to darken the sky, along with the lives and the spirit of people everywhere.

In February 1934, another tragedy would strike the Pfeifer family. Louis' Uncle Adam Pfeifer, who was 39 at the time, and his two sons, 15-year-old William and 12-year-old Gilbert, were frozen to death in another terrible blizzard. They had left their home on a Saturday evening to go into town at Ellis, just west of Hays, for medicine for Louis'

Aunt Maria, who was ill. While in town they had car trouble and took the car to a garage. They left the garage about 9:00 P.M. to return home. They never made it home.

A heavy rain had been falling that afternoon, and around 10:00 P.M. it turned to snow accompanied by high winds. A terrible storm soon raged and lasted all night. Their car went into a ditch, and there was evidence the three had tried to use stone-fence posts to get the car out of the ditch, with no success. They set out on foot across a field to make for home in the storm. A neighbor, John Denning, found the three in his field at about four o'clock on Sunday afternoon. The father and two sons were huddled close together with blankets wrapped around them. Louis' Uncle Adam was in ill health too and the cold was just too much for him. His boys no doubt stayed with him for warmth and never considered leaving their father alone in the storm.

The great irony is this storm and the death of Louis' uncle and two cousins came on exactly the same day that his own mother, Theresa, had been found frozen to death in another terrible snowstorm. The very same day, February 18th, only eight years earlier.

Another irony is that those two brothers, Louis' dad, Alex, and his brother, Adam, had married two sisters, Louis' mother Theresa, and her sister, Maria. Then each would lose a spouse to the deadly winter storms of the Great Plains—leaving only his dad, Alex, and Louis' mother's sister, Aunt Maria, to survive and raise their families. Yet, for both tragic deaths to occur on the same date, eight years apart, was an unfathomable irony. This terrible loss would seem to be bad enough for one year, and yet the worst was still to come for the entire Alex Pfeifer family.

By May of 1934, it was clear the wheat crop was going to be the worst in nearly ten years. The year before was the worst wheat crop yield since 1917…and a cruel drought had gripped the Midwest for many years, resulting in continued dust storms and the terrible toll they took. What crops survived against the drought were taken by a plague of grasshoppers and chinch bugs too. By June 1934 it was announced in the local newspaper that the previous 19 months had been the driest since 1895.

Farmers, bankers, merchants, and all others felt the economic effect of the terrible times. Many farmers lost their farms to foreclosures. Alex Pfeifer had already lost his farm back in 1932, but like so many farmers, he continued to live on the farm as a tenant and tried to work the land—to somehow survive and get back on their feet. The banks did not want the farms to stand vacant, and there were not that many buyers for vacant farms anyway.

The drought affected wildlife too, since food for them was also becoming scarcer. This led to a plague of jackrabbits across western Kansas. The farmers and local authorities were forced to organize massive jackrabbit hunts to try to reduce their numbers and diminish the damage to crops. It was reported the starving jackrabbits in many cases were just too weak to run away from the hunters.

Then there was the heat. It continued to break records day after day in the summer of 1934 and peaked on July 13th at 117 degrees—setting a new all-time record, according to

The Hays Daily News.

It seemed things just could not get worse, but the coming months would bring another tragedy to the family of Alex Pfeifer that would tear the family apart.

In October, their father, Alex Pfeifer, was arrested for assaulting their dear older sister, Martina. He was taken to jail and their sister, Martina, who was now 20 years old, had run away from home and lived with relatives of their dearly departed mother, Theresa.

It was a horrible time, with much humiliation for the entire family and terrible ridicule and scorn heaped upon the Pfeifer children by many other kids. Louis was very young, only ten years old, but he always read the paper, and that was how he learned what was going on with his family. No one would talk to these two small children about this, so Louis and his sister Jerry were left in the dark. They said things like they were too young to understand. Well, Louis and Jerry understood a lot more than they were given credit for at the time.

The Hays Daily News gave ongoing accounts of their father's trial in October 1934. A jury was selected and heard testimony from Louis' sister, Martina, that shortly after her mother's death in 1926 her father began to assault her sexually, when she was only eleven years old. She said he even threatened her with a gun on various occasions, if she did not cooperate and keep this a secret.

Louis' two older brothers, Gene and Fred, testified in defense of their father, and his attorney said it was all just the result of family quarrels. Louis never knew much, and understood even less about this since no one in the family ever really wanted to talk openly about it. There was terrible shame heaped upon their family, especially the children, who were innocent and did nothing wrong—yet so many people in the community treated them with scorn. These horrible times just drew Louis and Jerry even closer to each other. They were younger, and needed parental guidance and affection more than their older brothers. Yet, their sister, Martina, who had been a surrogate mother while they lived on the farm, was now also gone from their lives. This was the third time a "mother figure" had left them alone, and they were still only 10 and 11 years old. Now, they just had no one but each other.

Within a few days, the trial was over, and Louis' dad was found guilty on four counts of criminal assault. His attorney filed a motion for a new trial and an appeal. That delayed sentencing for a short time, but eventually their dad was sent to prison at Lansing State Prison in Lansing, Kansas. Now, Louis and Jerry were also without a father, who was going to prison for many years to serve out his sentence.

The trial was a sensation in the county. A great scandal and the talk of all the area. It was reported that there was standing room only at the trial. Louis, for one, was so glad when it ended. But he never really wanted to believe his dad could do those things, no matter what people said or what he thought he saw in those earlier days. Louis would always say his dad was innocent when he was teased and scorned by the other kids. Yet, in his heart, he knew better. Louis felt great sadness for his dad, his sister Martina, and his entire family. They had already endured so much pain, loss, and hardship. Louis often wondered in those times if life was really worth living or not.

In 1934, Louis was just ten years old. Up to now his life had been marked by two great losses and much sorrow that came with them. The death of his beloved mother, Theresa, in 1926, and then the death of his wonderful Grandma Cecelia Pfeifer in 1930, whom Louis and his sister, Jerry, lovingly called "CC." But with little warning, in this month, his life and the life of the entire family would take a horrible new turn.

Louis felt guilty about his dad himself. He did not know how to deal with this. One day Louis was walking in town, and his path took him across the street from the jail. Dad was looking out a window from his basement cell and saw Louis. He called over to him—"Pfeifer," he called. "Come over here...where are you going?" Louis looked his way when he heard his last name called out, but he ignored his dad and just kept walking. Louis felt so guilty to do this, but he was afraid, ashamed, and just had no idea how to cope with this terrible new situation in his life.

Marcel, sister Jerry, and Louis were kept with various relatives at this time. But after the trial and when Dad was sent to prison, they were staying with the deputy sheriff, Frank, for about one week. Well, one morning, on September 18, 1934, he just told the three children to get their stuff together and get in the car. Then, instead of taking them to school that day, he took off east on the highway and drove all day. Eventually they came to Abilene, and he drove to a high hill north of town. He then turned into the gateway of St. Joseph's Catholic Orphanage.

The sight of the imposing orphanage rising above the hilltop was overwhelming to the three Pfeifer children. It stood four stories tall, rising above even the tallest trees that stood nearby. In the center, a bell tower was even another story higher. Then, atop the bell tower stood a great white cross directing the viewer's eyes and awareness straight up into the blue sky toward heaven.

This looks bigger than any building in Hays that I ever saw, Louis pondered silently to himself. But his attention was also drawn across the road to the great complex of barns, with the massive dairy barn right in the center, running parallel to the highway. Louis liked dairy work. Even at his tender age of ten years, he was an experienced hand at milking cows. This familiarity gave Louis a certain sense of comfort that helped soothe the tension of uncertainty he felt as they approached this strange and imposing new home.

Then Jerry noticed the grotto to the Blessed Virgin Mary in the corner of the orphanage grounds toward the southwest. "Look," she exclaimed to her two brothers, Louis and Marcel. "Isn't that wonderful?" The boys did not respond, but directed their gaze for just a moment in that direction. Louis thought to himself that this grotto looked strange and mysterious. It was made of a curious rugged black rock that he had never seen before. It looked like volcanic magma or something out of the bowels of the earth...Louis wondered, yet he had never actually seen magma, except in pictures in the encyclopedia book.

Within just a moment the car driven by Deputy Sheriff Frank came to a stop and the three kids saw the nuns waiting on the steps of the orphanage to take custody of them. Deputy Frank got out and greeted the nuns. He gave them a folder holding papers and then opened the car door and told the three children to get out.

Deputy Sheriff Frank had never said one word to the children on the long drive from Hays to Abilene. Then, just as he was getting back into his car after dropping them off on the steps of the orphanage, he looked Louis straight in the eye and with a mean squint in his eyes said, "You are going to turn out to be a rapist, just like your father." Harsh words to say to a ten-year-old boy. But Louis' instant reaction was that he would be nothing like his father. It was a horrible, sad time. Louis was ready to just give up on the world and life at this point.

Chapter 17

Orphanage times

Louis thought about Jerry a lot when he was a prisoner of war in Germany. They had taught each other a lot of things. She was always his best friend growing up. She was a really good person, strong, yet gentle, and grew up into an extraordinary woman. They helped each other a lot all their lives, especially when they were young, Louis often thought to himself.

Jerry and Louis were so close, they were like one person. She did not earn any money in the orphanage, so Louis carried the purse strings. At St. Joseph's orphanage girls could not go into town, only the boys who did work at the orphanage. So they had an inside track, and Louis never failed when he went to town to bring her something. You could get three candy bars for a dime. Plus, they always shared everything with each other equally.

Louis milked cows in the dairy for St. Joseph. He was paid a dime a week for milking cows. The orphanage had a big herd, and it was part of the business end of the orphanage farm that helped support the orphans.

The cows were milked three times a day, morning, noon, and night. It was a big job. A big, strong nun named Sister Xavier Cunningham was in charge of the dairy milking operation. She was tough and always meant what she said, but she was also a really good person and never gave Louis a hard time. Plus, Sister Xavier worked just as hard as everyone else and always set a good example to the boys. She could see Louis knew a lot about dairy cows and was a very hard worker for his age.

All the cows were tested each month. The boy who milked and got the most butter fat for each month also got a fifty-cent bonus. Louis was usually the winner of that extra bonus because he knew more about cows than the other boys. Louis always made sure he got to milk the Guernsey cows instead of the Holsteins, because they gave more butterfat. Holsteins gave more milk, but it had less butterfat. Plus, he also watched the cows that were late in their lactation period, because they gave more butterfat too. So Louis always tried to make sure he was the one who milked them as well.

Sunday was the only day off, and their only pastime was to sit by the road and watch the cars go by. They would try to guess the model year of each car as it passed. Occasionally the orphans would get to go into Abilene to see a movie. It only cost 10 cents. There were always serial westerns and cliffhangers. Louis' favorite movie character was a cowboy called Bob Steele. He was not a big man, small in fact, but he was a great fighter! Louis was also small, but tough and strong—just like Bob Steele, his cowboy role model!

Louis went to so many different schools growing up. The teachers kept putting him back a grade or two. They thought he was not as smart as he should be for his age. Nor as well educated as he should be. But Louis was just not too good at school, and it was not so much that he did not know or learn his lessons as that he just did not give a damn about school. His chaotic life left him rebellious. Plus, the lack of parental guidance left little appreciation for how important a good education would be in this life.

Sister Basgall was in charge of the St. Joseph orphanage, and she was very strict—no monkey business! Once Jerry was being a little more than friendly with a fella her age named Willy at the orphanage. Well, maybe Louis was a little jealous of his big sister having another friend, so he sneaked into the girls' restroom and wrote in chalk, "Jerry loves Willy" on the back of the door. The nuns assumed Jerry did it! Louis had no idea Jerry would get in so much trouble! They even made her bind up her very small and young breasts since she was showing so much interest in boys at that young age. Jerry said that really hurt, to be bound up so tight across her chest that she could hardly breathe…but she never told on Louis. She just took all the blame herself. Jerry was all heart and never wanted to see anyone hurt, especially her little brother, Louis, even if it got her hurt instead.

Most of the nuns at St. Joseph's were very good, but some were also very strict. One nun was a huge woman with a strong and intimidating presence. She had a personality to match as well, as far as Louis was concerned. She never put up with any nonsense from any of the orphans. Well, Louis also had a crush on a girl his age in the orphanage too. And just to get even with Louis, someone else carved his and her initials in the girls' bathroom door. When the big nun saw this scratched damage to the girls' bathroom door, she got so mad she took Louis and his girlfriend outside and whipped them both with a short rubber hose. That was the worst beating he had ever had up to that point in his life. Yet, Louis always struggled to remember this nun's name in later years, but never could. Perhaps he managed to just erase her name from his memory in thanks for that beating!

But Sister Antonia was Louis' favorite nun. Since he was not too good in school and never went to one school long enough to really learn anything, she took a special interest in him. This was in spite of Louis' rebellious nature, due to his hard life so far. Yet, Sister Antonia was very patient, and she taught Louis how to study. He even became a perfect speller under her guidance and soon developed a big vocabulary too. Louis once even came in second place in a spelling bee!

Sister Antonia's name prior to becoming a nun was Anna Mary Dreiling. She was from Victoria, Kansas—just east of Hays. The Dreilings and Pfeifers were generally very close family friends. Perhaps for this reason Sister Antonia took a special interest in little ten-year-old Louis. It certainly helped Louis feel a little more at home at the orphanage.

The food at the orphanage was just horrible as far as Louis was concerned. It was always boiled vegetables grown right there in the garden. Jerry worked in the kitchen, yet she rarely got anything special for them to share. There was just not anything special available. They hardly ever got meat in any meal. The only treat was on Sunday when they would get pancakes and a dessert. But the pancakes were often lumpy with solid chunks of baking soda in the batter. This had a harsh metallic taste to it, and ruined the joy of eating pancakes.

In the southwest corner of the St. Joseph grounds stood that huge grotto as a shrine to the Virgin Mary. The children went to a Mass every day and then said a Rosary at the grotto. Louis often wondered how many times he said the Rosary at that grotto.

Fred did not have to go to the orphanage. He stayed with various relatives and just knocked around on his own. Marcel went to St. Joseph's along with Jerry and Louis, and was there for nearly two years, and then Gene got him out in June 1936.

Jerry got out of the orphanage first, on May 12, 1935, after only eight months when her Aunt Marie in Kansas City came and got her. She was 12 years old when she went to Aunt Marie's home. Marie was one of her father's younger sisters.

The departure of his sister Jerry to their Aunt Marie's home was perhaps the most stunning blow Louis had felt so far in his difficult life. The loss of his mother when he was only two years old was heartbreaking, but he was so young... the impact was measured by his lack of maturity. Then the loss of his Grandmother CC, a loss much harder to bear since he had known her for years and basked in the warmth and loving care she provided. Perhaps most jarring was the breakup of his family when his sister Martina, who had been his surrogate mother at the farm after Grandmother CC died, ran away from home and accused their father of abuse. Louis' father was taken to jail. The social scandal added a full measure of scorn and shame upon Louis and his family, which would take a lifetime to heal.

The first night Jerry was gone, Louis just lay in bed and cried. He felt such a lonely helplessness. He felt doomed to a life of hard luck and hardship. He was just consumed with sadness and despair.

After Jerry went to live with Aunt Marie, Louis and a little buddy of his started making plans for their escape from the orphanage. He felt so alone without Jerry. First, he lost his mother, then his grandmother, then his sister Martina left, then his dad went to prison, and now...even Jerry was gone! Heck, she was all Louis really had and the only person he knew he could count on, and now she was gone too.

Now, for the first time, at the tender age of 11, Louis felt alone—totally on his own, with no family around him. Sure, there were 30 to 40 nuns and maybe as many as 80 other orphans at any given time, but they were not family.

Later in his life, and now as a prisoner of war, Louis felt he had led a hell of a life. Louis often felt down on life, especially his own. He often wondered, what the hell else can happen to me? Now Louis looked back on those orphanage escape plans and laughed at how naive it was—we were only about 11 at the time. Where the hell were we going to go? What on earth were we going to do to get by? Well, their planning never got that far. They just knew they wanted out of St. Joseph Orphanage. As the years passed and he matured, Louis decided the orphanage was not all that bad. He realized they were trying to take care of so many orphans with very limited means and resources. At least the Sisters in charge would not shoot Louis if he was caught trying to escape, like his present German captives were certain to do.

Chapter 18

Jerry goes, Louis stays

After Jerry left to live with Aunt Marie and her family in Kansas City, and Louis was left feeling so alone, a flood of letters from 11-year-old Louis began to arrive at Jerry's new home. The first, dated June 4, 1935, read:

> *Dearest sister:*
>
> *How are you I am fine and hope you are the same. Is daddy still sick or is he getting better or worse.*
>
> *We got a letter from Martina we got quiet few lately. What grade are you going to be in next year? I think the house or the land sold for $400 dollars. Am I write or wrong. Please tell me what bought that much. We had a party Thursday night we could dance with any girl we wanted to I danced with pretty many of them. We got some good candy to. A lots of children went for summer vacation. There are quiet few new ones since you left. Do you think we get to go for a vacation this summer? Well I haven't much to say this time. So I must close with a lot's of good luck for you. Good bye.*
>
> *From your loving brother,*
>
> *Louis P.*
>
> *P.S. Sister Antonia and Omer said for me to say hello and me too your brother Louis.*

Another letter followed on June 18, 1935:

> *Dear Sister and all,*
>
> *I received your letter of June the 17ᵗʰ and was very glad to hear from you. We also received your package. What do you do these days since you get so lonesome. When you get to go see daddy tell him hello for us. Do you think we can go down to K.C. and see our Uncles and all relations this summer before school starts. I wanted to answer your letter sooner but we were busy putting up hay so we could not write sooner. We wrote a letter to Martina about 3 weeks ago but she did not answer it yet. Did uncle John Paul move because their address has changed.*
>
> *I get lonesome once in a while for my sisters and brothers and daddy when I don't have nothing to do.*
>
> *Dear sister I hate to ask you for a pair of shoes if you have any money to spare if not it's all right for I hate to walk barefoot this summer. So I guess I must close my letter for tonight for we got home from the sand farm at a quarter till eight. Tell uncle John and Aunt Marie hello for me. So good bye sorry I can't write more XXXX for John XXXXX for Aunt Marie XXXXXX for Dear sister Geraldine. Thanks for the gift I would like to see you all if I could. Good Bye, Louis*

Then again, only two days later, June 20, 1935, Louis writes:

Dear Geraldine:

How are you? I am fine. And hope you are the same. I was busy all week so I couldn't write a letter to you. I was just waiting for a letter from you. We are getting along fine in the hay barn. We are filling it with hay. But when Marcel brought one rack home it tiped over and I also broke the trip rope. After we were finished Sister gives us some candy and cookies. I am also learning to serve (mass). So I must close for this time.

Your loving brother,
Louis Pfeifer
P.S. Sister Antonia and Sr. Agnese and Sr. Omar send their best regards.

[Then, continuing at the bottom of the letter, Sister Liguori wrote this note to Geraldine.]

Love from us all, and may God bless you dear Geraldine.

You don't know how we miss you. I know you have a nice home, you must thank God for it. Sister Prudentia came last week and the first thing she said was, where is my Geraldine? Be a good child and God will bless. Don't forget to pray for me. Your sister Liguori

Another letter followed from Louis to Geraldine on June 30, 1935.

Dear Sister:

I sure was glad to hear from you. It seemed so long still it isn't. Are you going to take us for a vacation this summer. I wrote two letters today.

We also went to the show Saturday. We are going to Browns Lake July the 4. I think we will have alots of fun there.

When are you coming to see us. Did you have any big floods in K.C. We had some but not very big ones.

Sunday we played bingo. I got bingo once. I got a big pack of task papers, I sure had to laugh. Well I haven't very much to say this time. So I must close for this time with lot's of love.

Your loving brother,

Louis P.

Good-bye.

Then, continuing the stream of letters to his sister, Louis and Marcel wrote on August 31, 1935:

Dear Geraldine & all,

We received your letter of August 30ᵗʰ and sure were glad to hear from you again. We had our vacation and sure had a good time. Our school is going to start Tuesday. Dear Geraldine what did Daddy have to say to you. I wish I could see him. Geraldine did they have his trial and what did they do to him. Geraldine do you think we can come down to K.C. after school is out. I sure hope so. Geraldine we're saving all our money so I can come down after school if Uncle Johnny can't take us. Geraldine I wrote a card to you about a week ago did you get it. Geraldine is Alfred coming back to go to school at Hays. When Alfred goes tell him to stop in on his way and tell him I still got his ring. Soon I will send a picture. They're gonna have a fair in Abilene in Sept. and we'll have them taken and send them to you. Please answer all my questions.

Your Brothers
Marcel & Louis

The following day, on September 1, 1935, Louis wrote again:

Dear Geraldine,
I sure was glad to hear form you. When we come back from our vacation we will have plenty to write. I seen lots of our relations and our old home again. Yes, we had a good time in Hays. But I just couldn't believe that it was Hays. Until I seen some things that I could remember. I seen Deputy Frank but I did not talk to him. We are going to write daddy a letter in about two days. We had pretty much rain lately did you? We are going home Christmas again. School starts Tuesday so we have to get ready. I am in the 5th grade. Geraldine I can't send you any of my pictures till Eugene sends me one. I sure was glad to see my uncle Andy. We didn't like to leave Hays either. Well I must close for this time with lots of love. Good bye

Your loving brother
Louis P.
P.S. I was sick the other day but it is alright now.
I also have to milk a couple of fresh cows. Good bye
– oxoxoxoxoxox

Geraldine's (Jerry's) letters written to Louis during this period did not survive. But the letters from Louis to her, quoted above, were saved by Geraldine. In fact, she kept every letter written between her and her brother Louis all throughout the war. The bond between them as brother and sister was that strong.

Aunt Marie meant well, but she had a terrible temper and the fastest mood swings Jerry had ever seen from anyone. Jerry seemed fairly happy with Aunt Marie and Uncle Johnnie Paul and his family, except for the times when Aunt Marie got so upset with her. The longer Jerry was there and growing up into her teen years, the harder it was to get along with Aunt Marie. By September 1938, when Jerry was 15 years old, she and Aunt Marie were not getting along at all. Jerry, like most girls her age, was starting to show an interest in boys and wanted to look good. She wanted newer clothes but had no money of her own to buy them. The times were still very tough, and there was little extra money in the Paul household. Jerry pressed the matter with her Aunt Marie and they had a terrible fight. Jerry was very upset and considered running away from her aunt's house, getting a job, and dropping out of school. So she wrote her dad, Alex, who was still serving his sentence in Lansing State Prison, to ask his advice. He responded as follows:

> *Miss Geraldine Pfeifer*
> *K.C. Mo.*
> *Sept. 18, 1938*
>
> *Dearest in all creation: Must answer some of your letters that are as lovely as you are. First, I wish to know dear. Why not consult Uncle Andy about your going to school? Louis succeeded in climbing the ladder so far, why not climb the other two steps and have something secure for the rest of your life, which is only beginning?*
>
> *You are eligible for assistance from the state or county of some kind and should by some means receive the benefit thereof by handing in your application immediately.*
>
> *If you know how to forgive your aunt dear, I'm sure she will forgive you, and help you through school and every other incident. Or, you may say my dear, "What do you mean by this expression?" I mean this child, if you have a spiritual power and can develop it, your feelings will tell you because it is the greatest power on earth. No one beloved can wound us more deeply than a dear friend. That is what Aunt Mary is.*
>
> *Please dear, nurse no hatred against her, she has done so much for us, and is so important to us. She has, like you and I, her right in happiness.*
>
> *One cannot be happy alone. There is no such thing*

as selfish happiness. If you are big in heart and spirit you'll forgive her as she will you. Remember this dear. God made us all. Though he made and shaped each of us differently, we all have the same divine spark within us. It is the kind of intelligence we each must have dear, to have and keep peace on this earth.

Beautiful, the battle such as your Auntie expressed to me is so often caused by nervous tension than by temper! There are unnecessary tension makers in every busy day that can steal your youth and charm! Learn dear to recognize them – discover how to correct them. I know that you can out-wit those beauty robbers, if you'll be on your guard!

But you are still in the full flush of youth. Unaware of the tragic moral failures of the city. Aunt Marie knows well all the failures of the city and will guard you as your own mother would guard and pro-tect your beautiful, alluring personality and youth. Darling you are lovely, clean and innocent in your honest, girlish efforts.

But, as above stated, a girl's promise, of your age, is not enough for me, because if you open-mindedly examine the tragic tale of high school love that one can read in newspapers almost daily, you would not wonder why Daddy is worried about his beautiful child. Again my darling, as Aunt Marie and I, your mother would feel the same way about it, and guard your safety just as I, only more so.

As for buying winter clothes on the installment

plan, my dear, do not go into debt too deep, for should you run out of employment and fall back on your payments, they will take the clothes as well as the money you paid in on them. But, should you get into such a crack, you always know where to find Daddy.

Not alone for my sake dear. But for your own common good, stay away from Hays and everyone in Hays, as long as I am in this God forsaken place. There is absolutely nothing out there for you and your two youngest brothers and they will be living with me in K.C. as soon as I get out of here and established. But, please keep this confidential for the time being. It is my intention to settle our estate out there and sell oil rights out there and start a business of some kind of our own in K.C. That and many other reasons is why I would like to see you get an education.

Love, Dad

Jerry hung in there, and by early in the spring of 1939, she met the man who would become her husband and life partner. Meanwhile, Jerry was also compelled to quit high school because the foster care allotment money her Aunt Marie was receiving from the state for adopting Jerry had run out. Aunt Marie said they needed to save the cost of Jerry's daily streetcar fare to get her to school.

Their dad was still in jail for molesting Martina. There were a lot of relatives in their family that were jealous, very jealous of Alex, in spite if his present incarceration. He was always a successful farmer and bootlegger.

When she first left, Martina went to New Mexico and stayed with relatives of her deceased mother, Theresa, who really had it in for her dad. For a very long time no one knew where Martina was. But later on, a guy in Hays who was thought of as the village idiot told the family where she was staying. She was living with her mother's sister, Aunt Margaret, in Santa Fe, New Mexico. Louis and Jerry actually liked her very much. She always sent them good presents for Christmas!

It made it so much harder on the kids going to school. Everyone in town knew all about the scandal of their dad's trial and imprisonment. The first night Louis was back in Hays when Gene got him out of the orphanage, he was playing baseball on the field at Lincoln School when Deputy Frank called Louis over to him and again said, "You're going to end up just like your old man, a rapist, and in jail." Boy, he must have really hated Louis' dad, plus Louis and all his dad's other kids too, Louis thought. Maybe it was the torment like this and others that made Louis just stay away from school. But Louis did really regret that he never got to finish high school.

Jerry Pfeifer – April 1939

Chapter 19

Jerry meets Jack, love blooms

Jerry had met her future husband, Jack, one day when she was only about 16 years old, in the spring of 1939. She and her cousin, Alice, were walking down Summit Street near 20th Street on their way home from shopping downtown in Kansas City. They were both wearing matching sailor outfits they had just bought and looked very appealing.

Down Summit Street came two young men in a blue 1932 Ford. They stopped and engaged the two sailor-outfitted girls in a friendly chat. The girls accepted the offer for a ride home, after a spin around town. Alice paired up with Jack, and his friend paired off with Jerry. It soon became apparent to both men that Jerry had far less experience with boys than Alice—so Jack's friend suggested they switch dates. That suited Jack just fine. He had already been burned badly by a romance with a girl who had far more experience than he had bargained for…so to Jack a lack of experience was just the ideal.

When the evening came to a conclusion, Jack was inclined to get another date with Jerry and perhaps get to know her better. So, he asked her name. She said, "Jerry." Jack had known many boys named Jerry, but he had never met a girl named Jerry. Plus, it was the routine ploy for local girls to always give a boy a fictitious name on the first date, just to keep them on their toes, or throw them off the track, whichever was the case. So, Jack assumed Jerry was not her real name. Therefore he said, "Well, if your name is Jerry, then my name is JACK." Well, his real name was Vern—Charles Vernon, Junior—but since his dad was already called Charles by all who knew the family, his name became "Vern." But this did not matter, for the truth did not come out until it was too late to correct the name-ploy. "Jack" was introduced to all of Jerry's family by that name, and for the rest of his days, he was called Jack by everyone, and never just "Vern."

Jack got to know Aunt Marie and her temperament a little too well on his first visit to their home. He and Uncle Johnnie, Marie's husband, and Jerry's uncle/stepfather were on the front porch talking and getting acquainted. Jack heard a commotion out in the kitchen as Aunt Marie was yelling very loud at Jerry and her cousin, Alice. She was calling them "sows" and many other foul names. Jack had never heard such temper and foul language in his life. He walked into the house for a moment to confirm what he was hearing and to try to understand what was going on, then turned and said to Uncle Johnnie, who was following him, "I am leaving, I have never in my life heard such ranting and raving, nor such foul language from a woman. And, I will not be back!" Uncle Johnnie begged Jack to please just sit down for a moment. Jack complied, but was still prepared to bolt out the door on a moment's impulse.

Uncle Johnnie quickly went into the kitchen and told Aunt Marie that Jerry's friend was about to leave, and would not come back—and therefore certainly not marry Jerry—if she did not calm down and stop yelling all the abuse at Jerry and her cousin Alice. Marie relented, and then did something that shocked Jack even more than the ranting and raving. She came into the living room where Jack was sitting, fuming, and she got down on her knees right in front of him, and then she begged him to stay and promised she would never act like that again. Jack reluctantly agreed to stay, but said he had never heard such carrying on and would never put up with that himself, nor would he expect Jerry to put up with it either....

Jack and Jerry did get married a few months later in November 1939. She did drop out of school and they started a family. Jerry was only sixteen years old. Jack was twenty-two.

After Jerry and Jack got married and had four children, Jerry worked as a carhop at her first job, and smart as she was, became a manager for a drive-in restaurant within a few years. But the old adage that "only the good die young" was very true in Jerry's case. She passed away from cancer when she was only 54 years old, in March 1977.

Anyone who ever knew Jerry loved her. She was always the best friend to all, especially the neediest of people who crossed her path. She always had time, took time, and made time to be there to help anyone in need. People soaked up her radiance and love as if the sunshine came straight out of her heart through her warm, lovely brown eyes.

Chapter 20

Gene & Irene's

In August 1936 Gene had married Irene, and several months later, in October, Gene came to get Louis from the orphanage. He had already gotten Marcel in June of that year. But he waited until Louis was a little older and could be more helpful with the chores around his place. Louis was grateful to get out of the orphanage after being there for nearly two years. But Louis soon learned his luck had not changed yet for the better.

Going to Gene's home and living with him and Aunt Irene, Gene's wife, was a big mistake in Louis' life, he later felt. But he never really had any choice. Louis never had any choice about anything when he was growing up. He felt they just used him as a babysitter and he did all the really dirty work. Louis felt he was no more than a day laborer, not a member of the family. They got paid to take Louis as foster parents and were paid $60 per month. Yet, he got nothing, but more work to do, just like he was no more than slave labor. Louis now felt like he had become one of the "Knopke boys...or just hired help," as he and Jerry used to call their older brothers. Louis felt Irene had become his bitter enemy. She told Louis one day when he had upset her, "You will end up just like your dad, and you are no good, just like him!"

Irene always waited until the dinner table, when the

family was all together, to unload on Gene all the bad things Louis had done that day. Except he never sat at the dinner table with the family, which included Fred and Marcel, Louis' two older brothers. Gene had also taken on the care of his next two younger brothers too during those tough times. Gene clearly had his heart in the right place and tried to make a new home for his brothers. But Louis had to sit by himself at a small table in the corner. He was not family and not good enough to sit at the table with the real family. That was Irene's rule. It made Louis feel so bad, and his bitterness toward Irene got even worst, along with his behavior.

So, first thing at dinner each night Irene would start off by saying, "Gene, you know what Louis did today?" Then she would take off on a litany of things Louis did wrong, from her point of view. Louis' big brother Gene would just listen silently and keep eating. He rarely argued or made any comment to her. Louis was never really sure why Irene disliked him so much. She had a big family, and all of them seemed to like him just fine. Louis really did a lot of work for Irene and Gene, milked cows, fed pigs and chickens. One of his jobs was to go into Hays and collect all the garbage he could carry to bring home and feed to their hogs.

But Irene's big family would frequently come over for dinner. Gene and Louis came home one rainy day from an errand to another town nearby. Her whole family was there, all the in-laws. There were so many in-laws there they had to move into the larger living room to get all of them around the table. But Irene made sure Louis stayed in his place. He had to stay in the kitchen and eat by himself at the small table in the corner. Louis felt like he was so unwanted.

Louis' older brother, Marcel, also lived with Gene and had already been there for four months. He was older and could work harder than Louis, so Gene took him home first. Well, Marcel and Louis shared a bed in one room. Marcel got up very early in those days, before it was light, to do his chores. He kept a box of matches beside the bed so he could light a match to read the time on the clock at the bedside. Well, one morning the window was open and a nice breeze had been blowing in all night long. The shear cotton curtains on the window would billow out over their heads. But when Marcel lit his match to check the time, the breeze lifted the curtain again and it touched the match and caught fire! It was really amazing how fast the curtain burned... Marcel jumped out of bed and pulled the curtain down and put out the fire. They came so close to setting the house on fire that morning! That would have worn out their welcome at that house permanently!

Louis' dad was always good to him. Even in prison, if Dad got some money, he would share it with Louis. Once he even sent Louis five dollars. He told Louis he could do whatever he wanted with it. Well, Louis was not allowed by Irene to just wander around town, but Marcel was given that freedom...so Louis asked Marcel to buy him a new pair of pants. Marcel had to tell Irene it was a Christmas gift he'd bought Louis with his own money. Otherwise, if she knew the truth—that the money came from his dad—she would have taken the pants back and kept the five dollars.

Gene and Irene often took off for several days with

other friends. They went out of town and Louis was never sure where or what they did, but judging from their comments when they got home, it was all about drinking, dancing, and gambling. That was what a lot of folks did for fun in those days.

So, Louis was left home to watch the kids, milk the cows, feed the chickens…and try to stay out of trouble. Well, before she left, Irene made a lemon cake with lots of frosting. It was all she left in the house to eat! Then, first thing she did when they got home was to get the cake out of the cupboard and see that half of it had been eaten. She held the cake up in front of Gene and said, "Look at this, Louis has eaten half the cake while we were gone!"

That night as they all finished eating, Gene told Louis to go finish his chores, then put all his stuff together. "You are leaving this house and I am sending you to Kansas City to stay with your sister Jerry," Louis was told by Gene. Gene had a 1938 Chevy, and it was not very good in the mud. So, even though it had been raining all day and the roads were very muddy, he was still determined to get Louis out of the house and out of Irene's hair. Guess he just really wanted some peace from her for himself too. So, Gene drove Louis to the highway, on a muddy, rainy night, to catch the bus to Kansas City. The last thing Louis heard Gene say to Irene as they left the house was, "Louis is leaving now and it won't be no hair off your ass!" Louis felt he would never forget those words from his older brother to his wife. It made Louis feel so happy to think his older brother would take his side for a change. Now at last, Louis was free and would be with someone who loved him, his sister Jerry, and she would not mind having him around.

While waiting for the bus, Gene gave Louis a six-dollar bus ticket and a two-dollar bill. Gene said it was for an emergency and when Louis got to Kansas City to go to Jerry's house. Louis took that money; it was more than Gene had ever given Louis, and he kept it for a long time. He even went hungry a few times, but he was never broke again. Louis was now 14 years old, and ready to take on life on his own terms.

Soon the bus arrived, and Louis rode it all night and most of the next day to Kansas City. When he got to Kansas City at the Pickwick Hotel and bus terminal at 10th and McGee Street, he did not know his way around town. After all, this was his first time in any city as big as Kansas City.

Louis had the address for his Aunt Marie, and he knew his sister, Jerry, lived close by. So, Louis asked for directions to Aunt Marie's house. It was snowing very heavily, with about six inches already on the ground as he began the long walk across the hills of downtown Kansas City. When Louis finally arrived at Aunt Marie's home, it was dinnertime. The family was gathered around the dinner table eating the evening meal. He was cold, wet, tired, and hungry. The scent of the dinner meal was heaven to Louis as he approached the front door.

But as Louis knocked on the door and Aunt Marie came to the door, she did not ask him to come inside or even offer him a bite of food. Instead, she called to her oldest son and said, "Honey, Louis is here. Put on your coat and walk him over to Aunt Jerry's house. Then come straight home and eat your dinner, honey." Obviously, Louis realized he was not wanted or welcomed in their house either. His bad luck had not yet changed.

But within a few minutes Louis was inside Jerry's home with her husband, Jack. Before he knew it, Louis was taking a hot bath and then wearing warm, clean clothes. Then Jerry had fixed him a wonderful late supper of roast beef, carrots, and potatoes. As always, Jerry was there for Louis when he really needed her.

Jerry helped Louis get his first job in Kansas City. It was a state of Missouri government job with the State Unemployment Office at 1431 Walnut. It was also a quarter master's office. But Louis was not too comfortable with all the high-ranking officers there who always said "Yes, Sir" and "No, Sir!" So, Jerry helped him get a job at National Bellas Hess at 24th and Hardesty. First day on the job, Louis made a mistake that he never forgot. He got on the bus to go to work and the fare was a dime. All he had was a quarter, so he dropped it into the fare box and thought it would give him back his change. But no! The fare box did not make any change. So, Louis paid a 25-cent fare to get to work when all he needed was a dime. This taught him to be much more careful after that too. But the job was great. It paid $40 per month in cash. Louis only worked seven hours a day and had Saturday and Sunday off. He was always paid in brand new five dollar bills. Louis could not bear to break his brand new dollar bills, but finally got too hungry and had to break down and spend them on food.

Louis' new job was fun. He was an office errand boy and wore roller skates to help him move faster all over the building with messages for various departments.

Later on, after he had saved some money, Louis bought himself a new pair of shoes. But they really made his feet hurt while he was breaking them in all day. So, while riding the street car home after work late one night, Louis took off his new shoes and sat them on the seat beside him, so he could keep a close eye on them. Well, he was feeling very tired after a long day at work on his feet, so he was soon sound asleep in his seat.

When Louis woke from his nap, he reached down to take his new shoes and put them back on his tired old feet. But the new shoes were gone! In their place was a worn-out old pair of shoes. Someone else was now walking around town in Louis' new shoes...and he was still learning life's lessons and the ways of the big city. Guess his bad luck was still haunting him, Louis thought.

And just as Jerry had helped Louis find his way around Kansas City and get his first jobs, he always took care of her too. First thing Louis did when he saved some money was to take Jerry shopping and buy her a new dress. That really made Louis feel good—to do something like that for Jerry. They were so miserably poor when they were children.

In fact, Louis could not remember either of them ever once going to the doctor. Not for anything. Oh, they got sick all right. There was just never any money for doctors, or medicine, or whatever. And yet, Jerry never once complained. She never told anyone her problems, or complained, but was always willing to listen to the complaints and troubles of others and offer whatever assistance she could, even if sympathy was all she had to offer. She was so good-hearted.

Later, late at night, while lying in his bunk in the POW barracks, after being awakened by a particularly close bombing barrage, Louis found himself thinking about his time with his big brother, Gene, and his wife, Irene. Louis admired and felt gratitude that his brother, Gene, brought him to his home from the orphanage. Gene had already taken on the care and raising of Louis' two older brothers, Alfred and Marcel. But Louis, as an older, wiser, and more mature person, now realized that just a few months before Gene brought him into his home, Gene had married Irene. Gene was 21 and Irene was only 20 when they got married in the summer of 1936. There Irene was, a very young woman, taking on not just a new husband, but a husband with a ready-made family of two younger brothers. Then, added to this challenging mix came Louis, the unruly and rebellious little 12-year-old. Surely, Louis was a handful for anyone—he now realized that. Plus, during the next several years, Irene was giving birth to her and Gene's own children too. No wonder she was cranky toward him, Louis now understood. This realization helped soften his feelings about the harsh treatment he'd had while living in their home.

Chapter 21

POW liberation, at last!

It was good Louis could speak German. The people he was with included Dutch, American, British, and French. They were kept in three barracks, but never got together. Most of the Brits had been there since Dunkirk, for four years. These were their final work camps. They got their food rations once each week. The POWs worked six days a week. They got one shower each week. This was October, and it was the first shower Louis had had since he was captured in June. It felt so good to be clean, but it also reminded Louis of those early weeks, then the months of his time as prisoner of war.

Remembering again, the terrible ordeal, when the Germans just moved them around the countryside, and kept all the POWs packed inside railroad boxcars. They often left them sitting on the railroad siding, sometimes for up to three days at a time. Louis and his fellow prisoners were there baking in the hot sun within those steel cars. The Germans had more important things to do most of the time than deal with their captives. These boxcars were packed full, and they had to take turns sitting and standing, yet many became too ill to stand. The only break was when the POWs got out once a day to piss. A lot of the POW men had diarrhea, and they just had to sit in their own mess.

They were given water only once a day. Plus a thin soup that was next to nothing. The Germans would kill a horse and cook it down in a big vat—they ate all the meat and the POWs got this watered down broth. Louis and the others would save what few bones you got in their soup and just grind them at night in their teeth. Eventually they would just chew them up. Louis and the others got so hungry they would even eat grass.

In the city of Leipzig, the Germans accidentally blew up their own ammo dump. They made Louis and the others work day and night to clean up the mess. Very dangerous due to unspent ammo in the debris. A guard who did not like Louis—the POWs called him the Green Hornet—really made Louis work. But when Louis could, he would wander off a little in the dark. No one really knew where he was then. Louis came upon another boxcar full of foreign women. They were cooking food for some other group of POWs. Louis asked them for some "kartoffel" (potatoes), and a very kind woman gave him what she could spare without being caught. Louis stuffed his pockets. He asked her name and she said "Marjorie," and then Louis asked her where she was from. She whispered, "Poland…," but she seemed so fearful of being caught with Louis by the German guards that she shooed him away as soon as his pockets were full of potatoes.

But Louis never forgot her and her kindness to him in that desperate hour. They both put their lives on the line for one brief moment of kindness from one human being to another. That sort of thing had been very rare in Louis' life so far.

POWs got fed once a week. They would eat it all at once, or try to save some if they could. Some kept their extra bread under their mattress, but other starving POWs would steal it and eat it. They really had no place to hide anything. So, if they had any extra food, they kept it with them in a pocket and told no one. Besides, if they left it hidden somewhere in the barracks, they might be bombed and destroyed before they got back, along with their stash of food! Our Allied Air Force would just fly right down the railroad tracks and destroy everything in their path. This stopped all railroad movement.

Louis got split up from his buddy, James, long ago. Now there was not one POW in his group from his outfit. He knew no one in this group of POWs. Plus, the Germans made a habit of putting an American uniform on one of their own soldiers to fake being one of the POWs. They used this form of spying to try to get the POWs to talk, or learn what they could about escape plans, work resistance, rumors from new POWs on action on the front—whatever.

One British POW Louis spoke to said that he had been in the Bataan Death March, and when someone asked a Japanese soldier for water, he would piss in his canteen cup and make them drink it for water.

There were also some orphaned children in their POW camp. They lived in the space between the barracks. They were all starving, with big swollen bellies, sunken hollow eyes, a very pallid color. It made Louis' heart ache to see them, having been an orphan himself. But there was nothing anyone could do for them. They were mostly ignored.

Louis and the other POWs did not work for nothing as POWs. The Germans insisted they were not slave labor, and they actually paid them. A big sergeant who was also their cook would line up all the POWs once in a while and with a guard on each side, he would give each of them some German money. But the problem with this was, even the Germans did not want their own money. It was worthless. Plus, the German guards never let the POWs out of the camp to go into town to go shopping. And if they did, no stores were open, there was nothing to buy. Yet, even still... the German people did not want their own money! They pay us, but never take us shopping! Louis would wisecrack to himself each time he got paid, still clinging to his ironic sense of humor.

Leipzig was the city near the Stalag camp where Louis and his fellow POWs were held. There was constant bombing going on all the time, day and night. The POWs worked all day to repair the bomb damage. P-38s came over constantly too. They would bomb and strafe, and the railroad tracks would rise up like great arches in the air when a bomb landed near them. The strafing was the worst part if you were caught out in the open. The destruction was just amazing. Burning buildings and equipment was everywhere.

The Germans held a POW roll call every night. Yet, twice in one week there were escaped POWs missing. Louis got one of the guard's attention and told him how all the POWs worked very hard. They were starving and just needed more food. The only reason these guys escaped was to find food,

Louis suggested. He was always the one who would ask for more food. This, in the eyes of the German guards, made Louis a troublemaker. So, instead of more food, they gave Louis extra work to do on Sundays—his only day off. Louis would have to spend that day cleaning the latrine and shining all the German guards' boots. Louis and another guy named Katz, who the Germans seemed certain was Jewish. And because of Louis' big broken nose, they still suspected he was Jewish too.

Then one German guard, who seemed like a decent sort and spoke good English, told Louis not to stir up any more trouble. He said there were places they could send him that were much, much worse than this and he would not survive, no matter how tough or what great shape he was in—he would just not make it. "Believe me," he said with grave earnestness, "you will not last thirty days. Just keep quiet and do your work." Louis considered this to be good advice.

The POW barracks were divided into rooms with eight men to a room who slept in double bunks, with a stove for warmth, straw mattresses, and one blanket for all winter. The POWs played cards or dice to pass the time. They used their German money; it was all they had. But the sky was the limit. One of Louis' buddies was always broke due to the dice game. So, he would want Louis to stake him to get into the poker game too. Louis would loan him what he could. One time he deliberately let Louis see his hand as if it was unintended; he was holding four cards that looked like he had a straight. That straight hand had Louis beat, so he threw in his hand. He told Louis later he did not have the fifth card to make the straight, but knew he could bluff Louis out of the hand. Nice guy cheats, then brags about it to me—after he beats me! Louis thought to himself that life is so full of lessons about who you can trust, and what you think you know is not always what is so. Louis just laughed as he allowed himself a brief moment of humor in what was otherwise a "humorless" existence.

There was a POW collaborator within the camp. Louis was not really sure what he was up to but he never got dirty, or did any hard work, and always had a neat and clean uniform. He was never punished. At one point several POWs found pictures in his stuff of him standing with the German guards, posing all happy and buddy like. He was turned in as a collaborator when Louis and the other POWs were liberated. No one ever heard what happened to him.

Liberation came as a joyous surprise one morning in April 1945. The Germans had been more than a little nervous in recent days, and rumors were rampant about the direction of the war. The greatest fear the Germans seemed to have was that the Russians were closing in on Leipzig from the east.

So, this morning they lined all the POWs up for roll call. But this time there were several trucks lined up across the compound waiting for them. The POWs assumed they were being moved to another camp to get away from the Russians. But when the German guards dropped the gates on the trucks and threw up the tarps, each truck contained a machine gun and crew. It seemed very obvious they were going to kill all of the POWs instead of move them! Louis again felt the dreadful fear of sudden death. But the months of starvation, dull monotony, and forced labor, combined with constant risk of eminent death from many directions—left Louis and most POWs numb.

Yet, no sooner had this happened than a high-ranking German officer came up in an armored vehicle. He jumped out and had brief but intense conversation with the officer in charge of the POW camp. Louis was not close enough to hear everything they said to each other, but what he could make out was that while the Russians were very close, the American 69th Infantry Division was even closer, coming in from the west. The Germans were giving the Russians more resistance, perhaps because it was understood the Russians took no prisoners. So the Americans were moving faster. The officer mentioned something about "war crimes" and treatment of prisoners, and kept pointing to the west toward the American front. He left quickly and continued toward the west to the American 69th Infantry division.

Meanwhile, the German POW camp officer gathered several of his sergeants around him and held a quick discussion. At that moment a squadron of American P-38 fighters came over so low they barely cleared the rooftops! Then another and another—the sky suddenly just seemed full of American fighters. Gunfire could be heard now toward the east and the west. The camp officer left the area quickly and told the sergeants to surrender directly to the prisoners! Suddenly the captive POWs became the captors and guards! Boy, were Louis and all the POWs shocked and surprised...

but they quickly took charge and began to march their new German prisoners to the west. Toward the American lines, and freedom for all the allied POWs—at last!

Louis took a watch from a German guard when he was liberated. The guard tried to cover the watch. It was a very fine watch. But Louis simply insisted and took it anyway. When he got home, Louis gave that watch to his dad as a souvenir of the war and his POW experience. Louis' dad pawned the German souvenir watch for money—not very sentimental, Louis realized later.

The German guard with the watch Louis took also had very shiny boots. Louis said he wanted them. The German said no, and pleaded that he had to walk home to Cologne. Instead he pulled a chain off his neck that held a small German combined compass and magnifying glass made of bronze, used for starting a fire, and offered it to Louis. Louis thought, I will never get lost or cold with this little gadget, and he accepted the offer and let the German keep his boots.

Some people said Louis would not last three days in the war. But he made it to the end. When the POWs were liberated, all the German guards were put in a big open pen. Their guns were stacked up as high as a house. So, Louis went into the pen, smoking a cigarette, and found the mean German guard who'd tormented Louis—the one called the "Green Hornet." He actually asked Louis for a cigarette, as if Louis was his long lost buddy or something! Louis just took the half-smoked cigarette out of his mouth and dropped it to the ground and crushed it under his boot. Then Louis just stood there looking at him, as they both remembered the same treatment he and many other German guards gave to Louis and all the POWs. Louis reminded the "Green Hornet"—in German, which came as a great surprise to him, that Louis always could speak German—that they would have all the POWs out in the open pen and a guard, like the Green Hornet, would walk by smoking a cigarette. One of the POWs would ask for just the butt when he was finished. The guard would walk closer to the pen enclosure and take the butt and drop it just close enough so the POW could reach through the wire and pick up the butt. Then just as his fingers were ready to touch the butt and pick it up, the guard would stomp on the butt and try to stomp the fingers too. They thought this was so very amusing. "Not so funny now?" Louis asked the Green Hornet guard as he stood and just stared at him.

Eventually, Louis and many other POWs were returned to the USA and landed in Boston. Their new base was at Camp Miles Standish. The food was amazing and wonderful. The cooks at this camp knew what they were doing. They got steak and all manner of wonderful food. Louis had lost a lot of weight, but due to heavy manual labor he and the other POWs had to perform, he stayed fairly strong. Now, he got fat pretty quick, which they had been warned about after living for nearly one year at the starvation level. At last, perhaps things were starting to look up in his life.

Yet, Louis did not return home after the war the same

person he was when he enlisted. His happy-go-lucky spirit, combined with a jocular and ironic sense of humor, had been dulled by endless days of manual labor and monotony as a captured soldier. Plus, the never-ending stress of constant violence and possible sudden death took a very heavy toll. Louis had been determined not to change or become bitter. But his life up to this point had also taken its toll.

Louis had given this a lot of thought while he had so much time on his hands. He decided, based on his experience with people, that there were two types. The first, and best, were loving, caring, thoughtful, considerate, and faithful to their beliefs. These people usually put other people's interest first, even above their own. His sister, Jerry, and his Grandmother CC were at the top of this list.

The second type, which Louis felt he had known all too many of, were mean, selfish, and usually negative. These people always put their interest first over all others. These people could always be trusted to make harsh judgments of others, without justification, and were always vocal in expressing their negative opinions.

It seemed to Louis that so far in his life, the first type just did not seem to last as long in life as the second type. Maybe their goodness and giving just consumed them. Or maybe living in a world full of so many mean and negative people just made the good ones anxious to get the hell back to heaven as soon as they could! Louis smiled to himself with that thought…*heaven* always sounded like such a nice place as a child. Louis resolved that his choice would be to always reflect the goodness radiated from his sister

Jerry, and others who were so good, like his mother Theresa and Grandmother CC, and always look forward to heaven's reward—sooner or later.

Yet, the most important thing Louis felt he had learned at this point was to not rely too much on anyone else. The good and loving people were a gift, but they seemed to just disappear when you least expected.

The mean people will take all you have in life and spirit. They will just consume a person over time. Louis told himself the most important thing was to find the inner strength to be self-sufficient, depend on no one, and treat all with equal regard, love, and respect. But over all else, be able to stand alone and protect those who needed you and depended upon you, to always set a good example to all—both the givers and the takers.

Chapter 22

To trust, to hope, and to endure whatever comes...

The last time Jerry saw her beloved brother, Louis, before he became a prisoner of war was when she said goodbye to Louis, along with their brother Gene and their spouses, at Union Station in Kansas City. This was just a few months before D-Day, and it was the last leave in the United States that Louis was given before shipping out to overseas. From that moment until D-Day on June 6, 1944, Jerry and Louis kept in constant touch with each other through regular letters back and forth.

But from the D-Day invasion of Europe on June 6th, until August 4th—for nearly 60 days—Jerry did not know if her dearly beloved brother was dead or alive. This was a hellish period of choking anxiety and dreadful fears of loss of her most adored brother.

Yet, true to her rearing and values, Jerry never gave up hope—as if that hope alone, the strength of that undeniable love and devotion to the family bonds that tied them together and linked their mutual destiny, that love alone was strong enough to keep Louis alive, no matter what horror of war he confronted.

Sitting at her kitchen table, with her two small children playing around her, a son and daughter, plus another on the way, Jerry tried to suppress her fears of what could have happened to Louis. She wanted to have hope, yet she reflected on the losses of their lives together: their mother's death when she was only four, then her grandmother CC dying when she was only seven, her oldest brother Gene running away from home, then her dearest and only sister, Martina, also leaving home and accusing their dad of terrible crimes, resulting in his going to prison and the three youngest ones being sent to an orphanage, then only her to be taken in by her Aunt Marie, who meant well…but, well at least now she was married and living her own life.

Jerry wiped a tear from her eye, which was black, swollen, and bruised due to a recent disagreement with her husband. She had learned that he also seemed to settle his disagreements with his fists, much like her dad was reputed to do. Yet, she could not recall her dad ever striking her. Another tear came from the swollen eye, and as she wiped it away she winced in pain. Her little son Charlie had stopped playing and was watching his mother wipe away her tears. He asked her, "Does it hurt, Mommy?" Jerry smiled at him and shook her head no. Then she began to write what was in her heart in a diary.

Jerry wrote this diary to her beloved brother Louis, during the period from D-Day—when she had no idea if he was alive or not…until she learned of his status as a prisoner of war and had an address she could use to write to him:

Dearest Brother Louis,

Writing this account sustained me and at those times I felt I was very near you. I believe you are the dearest person in all the world. I hope you are glad God saved you for us. Good night, perhaps soon I may hug you.

Good night!

Also, upon Louis' return home I found out he was liberated on the day I said, April 2ⁿᵈ, not April 4ᵗʰ, as the government had stated in the telegram.

August 4ᵗʰ, 1944, Friday Daddy received this telegram: "The Secretary of War desires me to express his deep regret that your son Private Louis A. Pfeifer has been reported missing in action since June six in France. If further details or other information are received you will be promptly notified." s/ The Adjutant General

At first I was dazed. I had to keep reminding myself that this had happened in our family. I couldn't believe it was true. Every time I allowed myself to think of it my heart choked me. I tried to think every conceivable way to help you but it was all so hopeless. All except the word "missing," which gave us hope that you "might" be a prisoner of war, working with the French underground, hiding out, or maybe marooned somewhere by yourself or even with some members of your unit. I found consolation in the fact that you maybe had supplies enough to last approximately 3 weeks and that you may have your radio, knife, and carbine. Also maybe your parachute to make splints, or a book telling you what berries, bugs & animals were eatable. But this would make it too easy for the life a paratrooper is trained to live. I was tortured by the thoughts that you were maybe starving, suffering, and wounded, dirty and perhaps mistreated if a prisoner of war. I kept thinking also of your jolly humor & wondering if you still possessed it, or if hardship now possessed you. I kept praying you wouldn't lose your temper if they were mean to you. But hoped you'd bear it for the sake of your own life so that God would bring you back to us again. For no matter how bad they treat you, you can't get anywhere by losing your temper. They'll only…. [kill you!]

Last night I dreamed I had a letter from you, it was bad enough that I think I will always remember that dream. I also dreamed of and relived that terrible Good-Bye at the Union Station that last time, when Gene & Irene were with us. I'll never forget that October morning at the Union Station. It was so cold. No one had much to say. You kidded me and said I'd gotten the wrong time for the departure of the train.

August 15ᵗʰ – Allies invaded Southern France. August 14ᵗʰ Marcel wrote and said he joined the paratroopers. I was disappointed. I read in the paper today (August 16ᵗʰ) where a paratrooper had been missing in action since June 6ᵗʰ, "D-Day," and was now known to be a prisoner of war. Your fate to us is as yet unknown.

The suspense is killing... wish we'd hear one way or another—

August 18th – We received a telegram saying you were a prisoner of war in Germany.

September 21st – No address to write to. I wrote to War Department and asked if your address has as yet been received. I called up the Red Cross, no news....

September 28th Allies not doing so well. A division of British Paratroopers was lost trying to outflank Siegfried Line. It is not worth all the lives we are losing. Everyone optimistic, thought the war would end by October 30. No such luck. I wagered a bet with Jack on it. I won. The war, they say, will go well into 1945. Everywhere you read that paratroopers are doing great things, what an outfit! What a dangerous organization!

Marcel tried to join the paratroopers but was rejected. Daddy and I went to a P of W meeting October 31, 1944 at Edison Hall in the Power and Light Building. I asked Dr. Strong why we've received no address to write to you. He said it may be because you are in a hospital. Also he said that the telegram would so state if you were ill or wounded. Providing the telegram or cable from Switzerland so stated. Well, my darling, I must close and call the Red Cross and see about writing to you. Oh! My dear, how lonely I was on the 1st anniversary of your furlough. It seemed as though you must come home or

*I'd go crazy. Soon it will be 5 months since your im-
prisonment. It must seem like 5 years to you. I often
find myself thinking that soon you will be coming
home now. I never before believed how happy just a
"thought" could make one. Then when I come back to
realization—then only can I think it may be a year
or more and that year will seem twice as long as the
past one because at least we heard from you about six
months out of the past year.*

*November 6th, 5 months—you have been a pris-
oner of Germany. I have written my first letter to you
as a prisoner of war. I had to get form 111, a special
P.O.W. stationary. Oh, how I hope you'll get my letter.
There's not much news in it but at least you'll know
that I think of you & that I know where you are. I
couldn't rest until I found some way to write to you.
I haunted every agency in K.C. & Washington D.C.
I called Red Cross, Military Police, Provost General,
inquired at Y.M.C.A. and the Post Office & perhaps
a few others. No avail. The Red Cross finally gave me
this address:*

Pvt. Louis A. Pfeifer – 37497013
Interned by Germany
United States P.O.W.
International Red Cross Directory Service
Geneva, Switzerland, Via N.Y.N.Y.

*My darling, now I could fill in that vacant space
where you put the address, little did I know you would
ever have such an address!*

Please Dear God Let Him Come Home Again to us for I Have Every Hope and Faith that he Will!!!

It was on November 24th, 1944, the day after Thanksgiving that I had a card from you! I was so happy it seemed my heart was too big for my chest and it seemed something would break. It did, you can guess what. Tears the only outside way a person can turn loose. Well, now we had it. An address to write to. Your card was dated September 8th. Daddy received the fireworks from then on. First he received a card from you dated August 2, 1944. Then a transit address from the government. Then another address – yet none coincided with my address. Finally another address, this one like mine, #82460 – Stalag 4B—Germany. Then he received tobacco and parcel labels. Then another letter from you. How happy those words in your handwriting made us no one will ever know. Your writing never looked dearer. Daddy turned the labels over to me, they were quite confusing... I sent you 6 cartons of Luckies. Also spent $10.00 on a parcel of clothing and toilet articles for you. Daddy financed it. He said to get everything I could to you.

December 13th, I read in the KC Star where Germany is faithfully giving P. of War their food parcels.

We received your bonds for June, July, and August. Then we thought we'd better write the other in case someone might be putting his or her name on them as I felt responsible.

I paid for half of your parcel. December the last I wrote to Finance Division as they hadn't sent you your September, October, November bonds for 1944. I got quick results. They immediately sent your October and November bonds. But I had to write another letter before they sent the others.

Went to another P. of W. meeting on December 28. Found out a lot of information but wonder how much one can believe. The other day we saw in the paper where a German tank was captured with a parcel for American P.O.W.s from the Red Cross in the tank. No doubt a living for the Germans.

How we missed you on December 25th. I was so blue, I listened to Christmas carols 'til 4:00 A.M. in the morning. I called up Daddy and asked him who he was thinking of tonight (Christmas Eve) and he said everyone. He didn't know what I meant. Seems like I always miss you on an occasion like that so much more that it seems I can't stand it any longer. I wish I could take your place for you, honey. I hope it's not too hard on you. So long for a while.

Yesterday, January 6th, 1945 – you were a prisoner of war for seven months, honey. How my heart aches for you. Seven months is a long time in a P.O.W. camp. I think of you all the time. Include you in all my plans and think constantly of the "Day" you rap at my front door.

Well, darling, here on February 10th, 1945 and dated December 30th, 1944 – we received a card from you. How happy we were to know you are still alive and able. Every day that passes I wish for a card or some word of you. Over two months have passed now and no word. Three days before it was in the paper, I knew you had been liberated. (That is if they haven't moved your camp.) I knew how many miles the Russians were from you and that they would be most likely to liberate you. I figured you could hear artillery guns quite plainly and would know something was happening even if the Germans were not giving you the news. On April 26th the list of camps to be liberated was in the paper. What a joy, it was beyond expressing to see Stalag 4D shine out among them like a Gallant Star!!!! I knew it!!!! Just as surely as I know you will be home by July 4th. Unless your luck runs like it has practically all your life. I am not bragging now but I have been right about a lot of things in this war.

Marcel had a furlough from the Aleutians from March 12th to April 10th. His girl became engaged to someone else while he was gone. By the way, Louis, I saw Edna Garrison and she is going to marry Loyal Wise. I told her to call me sometime so we can get together when Louis comes home. We also had a call from Doris Paul wanting to know where Louis was. Here lately it seems the papers are full of atrocities, everyone calls and wants to know "Have you heard from Louis?"

I went to one of Allen's restaurants the other day and found out that he'd sold out and went to a farm.

I got to talking to one of his waitresses and found that she'd worked for Allen so I told her all about you and it made me so blue to be on "Your Corner" with the Montague "The Blue Jay Bowling Alley," etc. It was torture to be there but I got some sort of satisfaction out of being up there. I tipped that waitress as a tribute to you.

This evening April 28th, 1945, the news you could get all day was that Germany had surrendered! It was unofficial however. Then at 9:00 P.M. came the shock that there was no basis for the report. What a letdown....

I know that you'll never see service in Germany again for an article in the treaty with the League of Nations says "no repatriated person can ever be utilized into active service." That's one relief but there's still Japan.

May 3rd, 1945, Monday evening – They say "daydreaming" is a "visionary fancy." Well, I've done a lot of daydreaming. I am always imagining you and I doing this or that. Either you're coming into the house via the front door, or, when I hear someone knocking at the front door and then go to see and find no one is there, why then I'll think to myself supposing it is Louie and maybe he's hiding like he used to when he'd come to see me. Well at times I catch myself in such a deep thought that my heart starts pounding as though you were actually here. The other day I said to Jack, "What shall I do when Louis comes home?" So, he says,

"Talk to him!" (It's not funny—ha! ha!)

Well, I used to dream of the war ending and now it's ended in Germany, but no one feels any better, you really wish it were over in Japan too so our boys could really come home for good and not perhaps face death in Japan. I don't believe I could stand it if you came home and then had to leave again.

Every day people call me up and ask me if I've heard anything from Louie yet. Up to today my answer has had to be no.

Please dear God, if you ever did or intend to do anything for me, <u>Let this Be It</u>. I'll do anything in return. Please send me a letter or something from Louie to let me know he is alive and will be home. I'll never ask another thing if you grant me this one favor. Boys are coming home every day from prison camps—why can't you? Will your bad luck follow you all your life, or are you due for a break? You've got to be or life will be simply empty without you. Somehow I have a hunch you'll be home in June or maybe the end of May. Then again a voice in me says no! But surely that's the devil! "Goodnight, Wherever You Are!"

My Dear God, I thank you from the very depths of my heart!!! On Memorial Day, May 30, 1945, Daddy received a telegram which says you'd been liberated on April 4th. But I thought you'd been liberated April 23rd or 24th. I was wrong.

Today I was made happy but am too unsettled to know whether I was happier on the day I received my first message from you from Germany or whether today's cable gram made me happier.

I don't deserve this, it's the best thing that ever happened to me. I knew you'd come through. I was cheering for you – I had a feeling you'd come home today and instead got the cable gram. It's things like that that make you happy beyond words. Marcel had a ten-day leave so he's spending a couple of days with us. He will then go out to see Gene. He's going to spread the Grand News, and Grand it is.

Marcel was sincerely happy at the good news. It was this cable just like it was with the beginning of the war. Your imprisonment and your missing in action – I have to keep reminding myself that this ever happened. Oh the waiting I have done! But it was worth it. <u>Oh God, Deliver Him unto Me</u> – Good night – Perhaps soon I may <u>kiss</u> you <u>Goodnight!</u>

My Dear Louis,

I've always felt that you are possessed of the greatest qualities found in a human being. You are the dearest person in all the world to me. I hope you're glad God saved you for us! Thank you for being my brother—no better one was ever created – I love you and all you love—Mother and Grandmother would want that, wouldn't they?

Chapter 23

Alex Pfeifer, the final years

Alex Pfeifer had been sentenced to 5 to 21 years in prison. He was released on parole in only three years. One of the conditions of his parole was that he never again set foot in Ellis County, Kansas—which included the town of Hays. Well, upon his release from prison on parole, the first thing Alex did was return to Hays, and in July 1939, he married Maria Helena Sack, the sister of his deceased wife, Theresa. Maria was also the widow of Alex's younger brother, who froze to death along with his two sons on February 17, 1934—the same day Alex's first wife, Theresa, also froze to death only eight years earlier in 1926.

Then, for violating this condition of his parole, Alex was apprehended by the local authorities and promptly sent right back to prison for five more years. Then he was released again on parole under the authority of his daughter, Jerry, in Kansas City. By now, Jerry had married Jack, and they had two children. Alex lived with them for only a short time. He and Jack were sitting in the kitchen one day talking and drinking coffee. Alex was also chewing tobacco. He spit tobacco juice right onto the kitchen floor. Jack took exception to this action by Alex and told him to wipe that up—"We do not spit on the floor in this house." Alex replied, "She can wipe it up," referring to Jerry, who was also in the kitchen working.

Jack pointed his finger at Alex and said with conviction and in no uncertain terms, "She is not going to wipe up your spit, and you are not going to spit on the floor in this house ever again! Now, you clean up your own spit and do it now!" Alex did quietly clean up his spit on the floor. And then he left their house and never returned again.

Jerry forgave her father and always kept in touch with him. Perhaps much more than all the other children. Jerry had a very big heart and forgiving nature. Plus, she took seriously the many lessons taught her by the Catholic nuns, especially the expression from Jesus that you should "judge not, lest ye be judged...."

In 1972 Alex became very ill with throat cancer. He was hospitalized and on IV fluids only for nourishment since his throat swallow function was no longer working for him. But Alex never did take much food in his later years. He kept nothing in his refrigerator except a bottle of Tabasco. That was it! Absolutely no other food in the house, unless you counted the old jar of peanut butter sitting on the kitchen table. But he kept a steamer trunk full of warm beer and a variety of cheap whiskey on hand too.

In his final days, the doctors had restraints tied to his hands and the bed to keep him from pulling out all the tubes and IVs keeping him alive. He was ready to die and realized the futility of going to all those extraordinary efforts to prolong his life. Alex only wanted one thing before he died. He wanted one final drink of whiskey! So on one of the daily visits by Jerry and Jack, he asked Jack to sneak in a pint of whiskey to the hospital and give him a drink on his next visit. Jack was not opposed to helping Alex with this request, but checked with the doctor first. The doctor said it would not do him any harm, not in his condition, but it would do him no good either. But he could not swallow or take anything orally. The doctor told Jack to go ahead and get the pint of whiskey and bring it in, then give it to the nurses. He would tell the nurses to add it to the fluid in his IV drip. So, a few days later, Jack was visiting Alex and was asked by him if Jack brought any whiskey with him. Jack said he did several days ago and Alex was already getting it in his drip, directly into his veins. Alex got very upset and said that did him no good whatsoever! He had to TASTE IT—that was what he wanted and needed. So, Jack walked down to the nurse's station, asked for the pint of whiskey, brought it back to Alex, and gave him several gulps directly into his mouth. Alex could not swallow, but he smiled and rolled the whiskey around in his mouth, then spit it into a cup. "That's more like it...," he said to Jack, with his final smile.

Alex Pfeifer passed away in October 1972. The local priest refused to say a Catholic funeral mass for Alex Pfeifer, due to his sordid background and prison record. Jerry had a cousin who was a Catholic nun in the area, and they went to work on this priest, plus going over his head to higher church authorities, and he soon relented.

Alex Pfeifer was given Catholic mass and burial services and then buried in a grave paid for by Jack and Jerry.

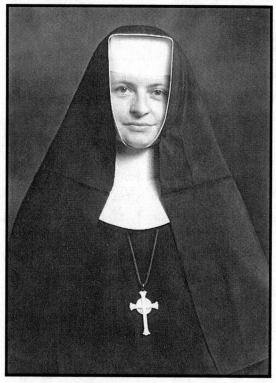

Sister Mary Vita (Martina Pfeifer)

Chapter 24

Martina becomes Sister Mary Vita

Martina, the sister of Jerry and Louis, essentially went into hiding after her father's trial and sentencing. She lived with relatives of her deceased mother in Sante Fe for a short time, then entered the convent at O'Fallon, Missouri, to become a nun. She joined her great aunt, Sister Beniglia Seitz, who was a prominent leader at the convent for this order of the Sisters of the Most Precious Blood.

Martina took the name of Sister Mary Vita and spent the rest of her life in the convent at O'Fallon. She feared her father, but was not bitter toward him.

Sister Mary Vita was loved and well-regarded by all the nuns in the convent. She was much loved by her sister, Jerry, and brothers Louis, Marcel, Fred, and Gene, who visited her as often as they could, once Gene had found her and organized a family reunion in 1960.

Louis visited Martina, now Sister Mary Vita, many times in her later years, to hear her side of the remarkable story of the Alex Pfeifer family and their early life in Hays. But he always remembered his first visit the most. He had a business trip to St. Louis and decided to take extra time on the way home to stop at the convent at O'Fallon to visit her. He brought her a gift of a box of Italian cookies from Vitales Bakery on the Hill in south St. Louis. The cookies were in a pretty white box with a ribbon over the box. She did not get many gifts or treats, so he expected her to be thrilled with the present. She did seem very pleased until she opened the lid to the box and saw it contained many colorful cookies of remarkable variety. He could see her smile fade into disappointment. So he asked her, tactfully, if he brought her something else the next time he came to visit, what would she like that to be? She raised her head, sitting right beside him, and looked him straight into his eyes through her thick glasses that made her eyes seem enormous, and said only one word with the greatest emphasis: "CHOCOLATE!"

Louis never forgot that funny moment. She was not joking. She was as serious as a stroke. The woman wanted, no craved desperately, the ultimate treat, the rarest of all treats in the convent—chocolate! When Louis got home to Kansas City, he express mailed to his sister, Sister Mary Vita, or Martina as he still thought of her, a 5-pound box of Russell Stover chocolates.

Martina passed on to her final reward in July 2004, within a month of her 90th birthday. She loved her family, brothers, and sisters. She loved life. She loved and served God. And, she loved *chocolate*!

Pfeifer Brothers Statuary – Kansas City, 1945

Alfred & Louis Pfeifer Statuary – 1945

Louis Pfeifer holding his Reindeer statue

Chapter 25

Kewpie dolls for sale

Times were still very hard for homecoming soldiers after the war. They had to scrape to get by. But Louis' brother, Fred, was always very enterprising, and had plenty of nerve and guts when the situation called for it. For example, he had learned from some of the best in Hays about gambling, poker, card dealing, and craps—dice rolling. Most of the people he learned from were his dad and uncles, so the talent seemed to just come naturally. But luck and skill did not always make a winner. In one poker game, Fred was sitting at the table farthest from the door and realized a cheating cardsharp was taking him for all he had. So, rather than go broke or try to leave the room gracefully…Fred just waited until most of the money on the table was out in the middle of the pot being bet. Then he reached out and grabbed all the cash he could off the table, ducked under the table (he was fairly small, so this was not a problem), and ran out the doorway! Well, the other gamblers chased him all night long, but to his luck, never caught him.

That event helped Fred finance the purchase of a Kewpie doll factory along with Louis' back pay from the army. Fred had already bought the plant during the war, and Louis bought in after the war. The plant was located on 402 – 406

Independence Avenue in Kansas City, Missouri. They sold the plaster of Paris dolls and other figures to traveling carnivals for prizes in their concessions.

Louis liked being in business with his brother Fred. He knew his older brother Fred always had a keen and shrewd business sense. He learned a lot from Fred all his life.

Plus, even though their working conditions left much to be desired—the place was damp, cold, and plaster dust hung in the air—Louis still found a creative outlet too. He enjoyed making new and unique plaster items. He even created a mold to make a reindeer with antlers...a tricky and delicate casting to make in plaster! But it soon became one of their most popular Kewpie dolls.

The business prospered and they both did very well. They could make 125 dolls per hour. They did so well, in fact, with this Kewpie doll business that they soon bought a big dairy farm on the south side of town together.

After several years of knocking around after the war and dating his fair share of women, Louis met someone that would become the love of his life. He was walking home from the Kewpie doll plant at the end of the day. A group of young women were sitting out on the front porch of an apartment building. Naturally, they noticed the dark, handsome young man walking down the sidewalk.

Yet, Louis was still fairly depressed from his lifetime of being knocked around by fate and the crushing violence and devastation he'd endured along with so many other veterans of the war. His happy-go-lucky spirit and jocular sense of humor had been greatly suppressed. He was not looking for love, or attention, and was really just minding his own business. Several of the pretty young women called out to Louis, saying such things as, "Hey, handsome, where are you going?" Louis looked up and made a half-smile, just to not be rude. His eyes instantly met one young woman's eye, who was not calling out to him. She was just looking at him. But Louis saw something in her eyes…a softness and kindness that seemed to understand, even if not know, that he had endured a hellish time in the war, not to mention his life prior to the war.

"Hello," she said to Louis. "Hello to you," Louis answered. She got up and came down off the front porch to the sidewalk and walked up to Louis, holding out her hand and saying, "I am Gilberta." The other girls on the porch teased and tormented the young couple with catcalls. Louis returned the introduction with his own name, and the two continued to walk down the street together.

This might have seemed forward, even bold to most men. But Louis liked her for it because the confidence and certainty appealed to Louis. This showed a strength that reminded Louis of his sister Jerry and the other women in his family who were strong. Plus, her obvious interest in Louis, without being coy or playing games like so many young women tended to do, or pretending to be shy and innocent—well, this also appealed to Louis, and he was flattered and impressed by her honesty.

Louis learned that Gilberta was more than three years older than him. Yet, given the time he'd spent in the war serving in the 82nd Airborne, Louis had matured to a level that more than matched hers. Louis also learned that Gilberta had a great deal more education than him, yet she seemed to greatly respect the other type of education Louis had—the school of hard knocks. The more they talked, the better they liked each other. Soon, love blossomed and marriage became a welcome destination for them both.

While Gilberta was a few years older than Louis, she was far less experienced. In fact, after dating a few women who were experienced, Louis had set himself a goal of marrying a woman who had no prior intimate experience with males whatsoever. Gilberta was that woman. Plus she was very smart and well educated.

As they became better acquainted and their love continued to grow, Gilberta heard more about Louis' experience as a POW during the war. She asked him once if he ever missed the company of a woman while he was a prisoner. Louis answered, no, not at all. He went on to explain that when you are starving to death, all you think about is your next meal. Nothing else but survival seems important. He said at night he would fall asleep chewing on a bone fragment because that was all he had, wondering if he would die in his sleep due to the constant bombing attacks, or just from starvation.

Then, after a moment of quiet reflection, Louis continued to say, "But now I do think about the company of a woman at night, before I go to sleep. In fact, that is just about all I think about…and that woman is you."

Gilberta smiled to hear his tender words. Their eyes met and held each other's, then they kissed and embraced.

Louis suggested they be married on New Year's Day so he would never have trouble remembering their anniversary—typical of Louis' sense of humor. But New Year's Day is a holy day of obligation for Catholics, and no weddings could be performed. So, they settled for the following day. Their wedding announcement appeared in *The Kansas City Star* – January 3, 1947 and read:

REED – PFEIFER

Miss Gilberta Reed, daughter of Mr. and Mrs. G. F. (Jobe) Reed became the bride of Louis A. Pfeifer, Thursday morning, January 2, 1947, in the Cathedral, Kansas City, Mo. The Rev. Father Byrnes officiated at the double ring ceremony before an altar decorated with Poinsettia. The bride was attired in a winter white wool ensemble with matching and black accessories. Her corsage was of pink rosebuds.

Her two attendants were her sister, Alyce Louise, and the groom's sister-in-law, Roberta Pfeifer. The former wore blue dress and black accessories and corsage of pink rosebuds. The latter wore a grey suit with black accessories and corsage of pink carnations.

Alfred A. Pfeifer and William K. Knoth acted as attendants for the groom.

After the ceremony the bride and groom assembled with the guests at the home of Mr. and Mrs. Alfred A. Pfeifer, brother of the groom for a wedding breakfast.

The bride is a graduate of Liberal High School and former teacher in this vicinity, has been employed as a junior accountant by T.W.A. in Kansas City.

The groom returned a year ago after serving three years in the armed services. A year of this time he was a Prisoner of War in Germany. He and his brother now own a business in Kansas City. The young couple will be at home at 1615 Central, Kansas City, Mo.

Louis' most beloved sister, Jerry, was not able to attend the wedding. She was in the hospital after giving birth on New Year's Eve to the fourth child she and Jack would bring into the world, a baby girl they named Patricia Ann. But Louis and Jerry were together in spirit—just as they had always been all their lives.

Louis felt very hopeful at this wedding as the priest said the marriage vows. His childhood had been anything but ideal. But he was not bitter, only hopeful and resolved that this would be a new beginning, and the future life of his own children, and wife, would be far more the ideal—he was committed to that goal and ideal, and resolved to do all within his power to make it so. As he thought this, Louis heard the priest say a passage he would never forget...the one passage the priest, Father Byrnes, said at their wedding ceremony, while reading from the *New Testament, The First Letter of Saint Paul to the Corinthians, verses 13:4-8*, that really resonated with him and seemed to sum up his life to that point:

"...Love is always patient and kind; it is never jealous; love is never boastful or conceited, does not take offense, and is not resentful. Love takes no pleasure in other people's sins but delights in excuse, to trust, to hope and to endure whatever comes. Love does not come to an end." Then, the profound words to Louis that his childhood was clearly behind him and a new life had just begun, from verse 13:11:

"When I was a child, I spoke as a child, I understood as a child, I thought as a child: but when I became a man, I put away childish things."

As Louis heard these words about love and the true nature of love, his mind raced back over his life and the true sources of love he had known. First, he remembered his sister Jerry, who was always the one constant source of love—unconditional and never-failing love.

Then, his mind turned to his Grandmother Cecelia, or CC as he'd affectionately called her when he was too young to fully pronounce her name. He remembered her promise to him, as she was dying, that she would always love him and look after him from heaven, as long as he would remember her.

Then, of course, his mother, Theresa—he was so young when she left and never returned, yet he knew and loved her through the great love and devotion given to her by his sister Jerry, and all his other brothers and sisters who did know her well. Plus, he knew her face and the love it seemed to radiate in the pictures of her kept around the family home.

So, as these thoughts raced through Louis' mind, he heard the priest say these words, as if they came from above,

"I now pronounce you husband and wife…"

Louis' head was spinning, so much was happening, this was so important—so special—as he turned to face Gilberta and their eyes met, then their lips met, in that first kiss as husband and wife. Louis wondered if he might faint, he was feeling so elated and even lightheaded.

Louis and Gilberta then turned to face the very small congregation that had gathered to witness their wedding. As they looked toward those attending, Louis' eyes were drawn toward something emerging from the shadows up in the choir loft. He quickly strained his eyes to try to make out what it was…it seemed to be a woman, about 30, dressed in a gown of silvery-white satin, yet still the color of the shadows. Then another woman emerged from the shadows, standing just behind the first—a larger, older woman, perhaps 60 years old…. Louis turned his eyes toward Gilberta's eyes and motioned with his eyes upward toward the choir loft so she could also see the two new guests observing their wedding. Gilberta looked up…then back to Louis with a question of "what?" in her eyes. She did not see them! Louis realized this as he turned his eyes again to the choir loft. Nothing was there…but only the dark shadows now. Then Louis felt a sudden shiver, overtaken by a rush of the greatest sense of love surrounding him, as if he was being fully embraced by his grandmother CC and his mother Theresa. His heart seemed to race and leap for joy! Louis smiled to himself as he said in his mind and felt in his heart, *I will remember you—always!*

Louis & Gilberta Pfeifer, newly weds, January 1947

Afterword

After they married, Louis and Gilberta raised five fine children, who are all a credit to society. For the majority of his married life, Louis owned farms, mainly dairy farms. He knew dairy cattle and liked that work. He also kept many side jobs too—to help make ends meet. Later in life he bought and ran a drive-in restaurant in Pleasanton, Kansas. Louis had also worked many jobs as a cook in his younger days and was very comfortable in this business.

Louis lost Gilberta to cancer in April 1995, and he never got over the loss. Those final years alone were perhaps as tough as his childhood years had been. But he never lost his sense of humor or determined spirit to see the best in people. He passed away in November 2006 at the age of 82 years.

His beloved sister, Geraldine Theresa Pfeifer-Needham, passed away on March 6, 1977. During her final months she insisted no one be told about her struggle with cancer. She did not want to worry or upset any of her loved ones. As always, she put everyone else's feelings above her own needs. It was not until she was near the end that she allowed her loved ones to know and come to her to say goodbye. Her only regret was she felt she had little to show for her life and would not be remembered. She was so mistaken. . . .

Jerry was only 54 years of age, and left behind a grateful

army of beloved family and friends.

Yet, again, Louis was alone, and each woman who had loved him, and he loved in return—mother, grandmother, sister, and wife—each the most wonderful and loving woman a person could know, all passed in the untimely, and all too soon, time of life.

Before she died, Louis was given a collection of letters and memorabilia from his sister Jerry of the times of their lives. The letters went all the way back to their days at the orphanage and continued during his time as a prisoner of war. Louis wrote Jerry a letter to express his gratitude and closed it with this expression:

To my most sincere and best friend, My Sister! With indescribable Gratitude!

Always,
Your Brother – Louis

Sources

This book is a work of creative nonfiction. By this, it is meant to tell a story based on real events and real people, but with certain creative license taken to allow the imagination to fill in the gaps in the story that cannot be otherwise known.

I first heard from my own mother, Jerry, that she had a long-lost sister, who it was presumed had joined a convent after she ran away from home a very long time ago. I was only ten years old. My mother's love for her long-lost sister was so profound in the telling of this story that, even at that tender age, I acquired an undeniable determination to learn all I could and then to someday tell this remarkable story. The more I learned over the years, the more remarkable this family, and the times during which they came of age, clearly were.

Thus, my first source was my mother, Geraldine Theresa (Jerry) Pfeifer-Needham. Then, the next source was to be my uncle Louis Pfeifer, who over the years rarely shared his war stories. Like so many veterans of the second World War, the memories were haunted by the great losses and hardships they endured. Plus, the respect they had for those comrades who did not come home, those less fortunate than them, who were somehow honored in their silence. However, later in his life and during his final years, I often met with my uncle Louis and he allowed me to interview him in depth about his life and times. Those interviews are the core and essential framework of this story.

Another very important source was my Aunt Martina Pfeifer, or Sister Mary Vita as she became known in the convent, when she was received as a novice into the Sisters of the Most Precious Blood, O'Fallon, Missouri. I was able to visit her several times too before she left this earth. She was fairly forthcoming in her memories for someone who had lived the totally cloistered life of a nun. The early memories, if not faded, were deeply buried and only slowly revealed in the occasional insight.

Other family members contributed fragments along the way, and I was always alert to learn all I could about their lives and times. This was our family history, and I felt it was worth knowing and hopefully remembering.

The next most important source was reading countless issues of *The Ellis County News* and *The Hays Daily News* from the early 1920s to the mid-1930s. These newspapers faithfully chronicled the events of the days and lives of those living in Ellis County, Kansas.

Other material that was so important in researching this story included *The Volga-German Pfeifer Ancestors & Descendants*, a comprehensive genealogy study by Anthony J. Leiker, plus these books that revealed so much about the culture and history of the Volga-Germans, and other groups, who settled across the central plains, including: *The Worst Hard Time*, by Timothy Egan; *Farming the Dust Bowl*, by Lawrence Svobida; *Rooted in Dust*, by Pamela Riney-

Kehrberg; *The Children's Blizzard*, by David Laskin; *Kansas, The History of the Sunflower State, 1854-2000*, by Craig Miner; *A Social Study of the Russian German*, by Hattie Plum Williams; *Heritage of Kansas, Special Issue – The Volga Germans*, edited by Richard Keller; *From the Steppes to the Prairies*, by Msgr. George P. Aberle; *Sei Unser Gast "Be Our Guest" – A Collection of German Russian Recipes*, from the North Star Chapter of The American Historical Society of Germans from Russia; *American Windmills*, by T. Lindsay Baker; *Sound and Fury: A History of Kansas Tornados, 1854 – 2008*, by Daniel C. Fitzgerald; and *Kansas in The Great Depression*, by Peter Fearon.

The following books on military history of World War II also provided valued insights into the historic events involving the 82nd Airborne Division: *Strike and Hold, A Memoir of the 82nd Airborne in World War II*, by T. Moffatt Burriss; *Airborne, World War II Paratroopers in Combat*, by Julie Guard; *All American, All the Way – The Combat History of the 82nd Airborne Division in World War II*, by Phil Nordyke; *The Encyclopedia of Aircraft of WWII*, edited by Paul Eden; *The All Americans in World War II – A Photographic History of the 82nd Airborne Division at War*, by Phil Nordyke; *507th Parachute Infantry Regiment – 1942 to 1945*, by Dominique Francois; and *We Were Each Other's Prisoners*, by Lewis H. Carlson.

Acknowledgements

First my mother, Geraldine, or Jerry as she was known to all who knew and loved her, has the foremost debt of appreciation and gratitude that is owed in writing this book. I cannot remember a time in my life when the stories of her life growing up in western Kansas did not capture my heart and imagination. I was in the fourth grade when she first told me she had a long-lost sister who had run away from home to become a nun. It was about this time that I began to imagine that one day I would write these stories down so future generations would also know them, and hopefully, find them worth remembering.

Then, to my daughter, Angela Marie-Noelle, who was born after my mother's passing and is the future generation and has been my constant source of inspiration and determination that these stories would be known and remembered—I am so indebted.

Plus, my two other daughters, Susanne Michelle, who not only assisted in editing this manuscript but reinforces in her daily life the determined and committed sense of family love, which she and her sister, Lisa Marie, learned directly from their grandmother, my mother Jerry.

Suella and Lawrence Walsh, who provided editing and proofing assistance, are also owed a full measure of appreciation.

To my sister, Patricia Ann, who shared with me a lifetime of love and reverence for these stories and memories of our mother, Jerry, and her boundless love for her brother Louis and the rest of her family—all of whom endured such great hardships, yet survived to be successful and commendable parents and citizens—I extend my heartfelt thanks. Her constant support and encouragement has been invaluable.

Last, but foremost, is my wife, Nona Jo Fowler—who brought constant faith, love, and understanding to this project, as well as invaluable feedback and editing assistance.

This work would not exist without them and so many others who also believed in me and agreed that this story was worth knowing and remembering.

CPSIA information can be obtained at www.ICGtesting.com
Printed in the USA
LVOW05s0133181113

361619LV00001B/1/P

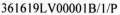

9 781432 771362